The Shepherd

Reflections on Psalm 23

Unless otherwise specified, all Scriptures are taken from the King James Version of the Holy Bible.

The Shepherd
© 2021 Beacon Street Press

Printed in the United States of America

ISBN 1-933641-59-2

The Shepherd

Reflections on Psalm 23

James Collins

To my Shepherd,
    Thank You, Jesus, for saving my soul.

To Elouise, my mother,
    Goodness and mercy followed her all the days of her life,
and she dwells in the house of the Lord forever.

Acknowledgements

I am grateful to the staff of Southwest Radio Ministries for their support and daily inspiration. Thanks to Chris Enders for helping me with the title for this book. Thank you, Donna Smith, for keeping things running. Many thanks to Edward Webber, Danny Phillips, and Tabitha Cook for laughing at my jokes and bringing donuts. Much appreciation goes to Christi Killian, Alan Joy, and Veronica Pemberton for teaching me all about design, layout, and printing. Thank you, Matthew McElvany, for your production assistance. Thanks to Mimi Davis for always having a kind word. Much appreciation to Kenneth Hill and Matthew Hill for your leadership and guidance. Thanks so much, Marvin McElvany, for fixing my mistakes and your production expertise. I am especially grateful to Dr. Larry Spargimino for your years of mentorship and guidance.

To my wife, Amanda, and my children, Abby, Timothy, and John. Thank you for allowing me to take the time necessary to write for the Lord.

I thank God for all of you.

—James Collins

Table of Contents

The Cross, Crook, and Crown

> *The LORD is my shepherd; I shall not want.*
> *He maketh me to lie down in green pastures:*
> *he leadeth me beside the still waters.*
> *He restoreth my soul:*
> *he leadeth me in the paths of righteousness for his name's sake.*
> *Yea, though I walk through the valley of the shadow of death,*
> *I will fear no evil: for thou art with me;*
> *thy rod and thy staff they comfort me.*
> *Thou preparest a table before me in the presence of mine enemies:*
> *thou anointest my head with oil;*
> *my cup runneth over.*
> *Surely goodness and mercy shall follow me all the days of my life:*
> *and I will dwell in the house of the Lord for ever.*
>
> —Psalm 23

Dr. Larry Walker, who was a professor of Old Testament and Semitic Languages at Southwestern Baptist Theological Seminary, once shared a story about working in the Highlands of Central America. He went there to translate the Bible into a very obscure language. The tribal people who spoke the obscure language had never seen a sheep. This caused a problem for Dr. Walker when he translated the Twenty-third Psalm. Since the villagers had no knowledge of sheep, they did not understand the meaning of the word "shepherd." Eventually, Dr. Walker came up with a way to get the idea across in a way the people would understand. He translated "the Lord is my shepherd" as "the Lord is my chicken-keeper." It is amazing to think that there are people in this world who have never seen sheep.

Truthfully, even though I have seen sheep, I don't know very much about them. Sheep were scarce where I grew up in Oklahoma. There were plenty of cows, but there were not very many sheep. As I understand it, back in the 1800s when Southeast Oklahoma was settled, there were bad feelings between the cattle ranchers and the sheep ranchers over fences. It seems that the cattlemen won out, so there were few sheep where I grew up.

However, I was in the Future Farmers of America, the FFA, when I was in high school. One of my friends raised sheep as show animals in the FFA. I have also been to the Oklahoma State Fair, and I saw sheep in the fair barn. Oh, and occasionally, I have eaten lamb chops. Still, none of that makes me an expert on sheep. I really don't know very much about sheep.

I have discovered, that even though sheep have not been an important part of my life, they are an important part of the lives of a lot of people. Did you know that sheep are one of the few livestock animals that are found everywhere in the world? Sheep are raised on every continent except Antarctica. In the Western United States, there are some states where there are more sheep than people. Australia has ten times more sheep than people. In New Zealand, there are twenty sheep for every one person. That's a lot of sheep.

Even though I don't know much about sheep, I own clothes made from wool. I still have some green Army-issued wool socks from my time in the military. Chances are, you also probably own some clothes made from wool. Even though you may also not know much about sheep.

Although we may not know much about sheep, we probably know something about the sheep Psalm. The Twenty-third Psalm is one of the most familiar, famous, and loved passages in the entire Bible. The Twenty-third Psalm is the best-known chapter in the Bible. Other than John 3:16, the Psalm 23 is probably the best-known passage in the Bible.

I believe the Twenty-third Psalm is so well-loved because life is complicated. Sometimes we are pre-trib, other times we are mid-trib, and even post-trib. I'm not referring to ideas as to the timing of the Rapture in biblical prophecy. I mean trials and troubles—that kind of tribulation. Someone reading this is just beginning to face trouble. Someone else is smack dab in the middle of a big mess. Someone else just emerged from a painful episode in life. That is why this psalm is so universal. It speaks to our trials and tribulations. It is a psalm for all of life.

Psalm 23 is the psalm of psalms. It is the sweetest psalm of all. There is no greater picture of the relationship that God has with His people than the picture in the

Twenty-third Psalm—the picture of the shepherd and his sheep. These words have comforted many heavy hearts, dried many tears, bandaged many wounds, given courage to the living, and comforted the dying. It is a psalm for all of life.

One of the first things that I remember as a child was learning the Twenty-third Psalm in Sunday school. Little children memorize these words. These are also the words people often whisper near the end of their life. It is a psalm for all of life.

I once officiated a wedding where the bride and the groom read the Twenty-third Psalm. The couple read it with a sense of excitement and anticipation. It is a psalm for all of life.

In a time of loss, we have all turned to the Twenty-third Psalm. I have used the Twenty-third Psalm at many memorial services, funerals, and graveside services. The words have been a source of comfort to the hurting in a time of deep and terrible grief. Even though the Twenty-third Psalm is usually read at funeral services, the psalm itself says that it is for all the days of our life. It is a psalm for all of life.

The Twenty-third Psalm is a psalm of David, and it was written over three thousand years ago. Even though this ancient poem was written long ago, it is up-to-date and current for the day in which we live. It is timeless. It is a psalm for all of life.

It begins with the words, "The LORD" and it ends with "the LORD forever." It starts with the Lord, and it ends with the Lord forever. It is a psalm for all of life … even your life after this one.

The Cross

The Twenty-third Psalm is set in the middle of three messianic psalms that present the coming work of the Messiah. Psalm 22, Psalm 23, and Psalm 24 are a triad of truth. Psalm 22 presents the Messiah as the Savior. Psalm 23 presents the Messiah as the Shepherd. Psalm 24 presents the Messiah as Sovereign. The focus of Psalm 22 is the cross. The focus of Psalm 23 is the crook. The focus of Psalm 24 is the crown.

Psalm 22 has come to be known as the "Psalm of the Cross." It is an amazing prophecy. One thousand years before Jesus went to the cross of Calvary, David described in graphic detail the crucifixion as if he, himself, hung on the cross.

Look at the opening words of Psalm 22, *"My God, my God, why hast thou forsaken me?"* Do those words sound familiar? They are the same words that Jesus cried from the cross. In Matthew 27:47, we read, *"And about the ninth hour Jesus cried with a loud voice, saying, Eli, Eli, lama sabachthani? that is to say, My God, my God, why hast thou forsaken me?"* When Jesus took the sins of the world upon Himself so that those sins could be judged and justified through His sacrifice, God in His holiness had to turn away.

In the Twenty-second Psalm, David described Roman crucifixion hundreds of years before the Romans even came on the scene. In the days when Jewish executions were accomplished by stoning, the psalmist described the sufferings of the cross. He described the people beneath the cross gathered to laugh at Jesus: *"... All they that see me laugh me to scorn"* (v. 7). He described the profuse perspiration caused by intense suffering: *"... I am poured out like water."* He described His bones as being *"... out of joint."* He described the action of the effects of the crucifixion on the heart: *"... my heart is like wax; it is melted"* (v. 14). He described Christ's exhaustion: *"... My strength is dried up."* He described the Lord's extreme thirst: *"... my tongue cleaveth to my jaws"* (v. 15). He described Jesus being nailed to the cross: *"... they pierced my hands and my feet"* (v. 16). He described the shame as the crowd gawked at the Messiah's unclothed body: *"... I may tell all my bones: they look and stare upon me"* (v. 17). He described the soldiers gambling: *"... They part my garments among them, and cast lots upon my vesture"* (v. 18). David wrote these descriptions a thousand years before the crucifixion of Jesus.

Jesus said in John 10:11, *"I am the good shepherd: the good shepherd giveth his life for the sheep."* When the Lord said those words, He spoke of His coming substitutionary death on the cross. This is the picture of Jesus in the Twenty-second Psalm. He is the Good Shepherd who gives His life for His sheep.

The Crook

Psalm 23 is the "Shepherd's Psalm." It is a beautiful picture of the Shepherd who cares for His flock, leads us through the meadow, feeds us in green pastures, and quenches our thirst beside still waters. Even when we walk through the valley of the shadow of death, we need not fear because our Shepherd is there to comfort us.

The writer of Hebrews described the Shepherd of Psalm 23 when he wrote, *"Now the God of peace, that brought again from the dead our Lord Jesus, that great shepherd of the sheep, through the blood of the everlasting covenant."* The Good Shepherd of John 10 is now called the Great Shepherd. Notice also that the writer of Hebrews referenced the resurrection of Jesus Christ. This is the picture of Jesus in the Twenty-third Psalm. He is the Great Shepherd, raised from the dead through the blood of the everlasting covenant, who tenderly cares for His sheep.

The Crown

Psalm 24 is also known as the "Psalm of the King of Glory" and it describes the coronation of the Messiah. The final verses of this psalm describe the triumphant return of Jesus Christ. In Psalm 24:9–10, we read, *"Lift up your heads, O ye gates; even lift them up, ye everlasting doors; and the King of glory shall come in. Who is this King of glory? The LORD of hosts, he is the King of glory. Selah."* The Twenty-fourth Psalm foreshadows the establishment of the Millennial Reign of Christ when Jesus will return and enter Jerusalem as the "King of Glory." It is a prophetic psalm that will ultimately be fulfilled when Jesus Christ returns to earth in power and in great glory.

The Apostle Peter wrote to encourage faithful church leaders with these words, *"And when the chief Shepherd shall appear, ye shall receive a crown of glory that fadeth not away"* (1 Peter 5:4). Here, Peter assured faithful ministers that they will be rewarded when the Lord Jesus Christ returns. The Great Shepherd of Hebrews 13 is now referred to as the "Chief Shepherd." This is the picture of Jesus in the Twenty-fourth Psalm. He is the Chief Shepherd, who owns the sheep. When He comes, He will establish His throne. We who have served Him will rule and reign with Him for a thousand years.

Psalm 22 speaks of our past—of our sins being forgiven on the cross. Psalm 23 speaks of our present life on earth. Psalm 24 speaks of our future in the coming Millennial Kingdom of Christ.

Psalm 22 takes place on Mount Calvary in the past where they crucified the Lord. Psalm 24 takes place in the future on Mount Zion where He is coming back to rule and reign. Psalm 23 takes place in the present in this life in the valley in between the two mountains.

If you are a believer in Jesus Christ, you live—right now—the Psalm 23 life. From one sheep to another, I want you to know that you can trust the Shepherd to get you through the valley.

In the book *God's Psychiatry,* Pastor Charles Allen wrote about the power contained in the words of Psalm 23. Allen recalled the story of a man who came to see him years earlier for counseling. The man suffered with tension, stress, nervousness, and worry. Doctors were unable to help him. So, the physicians sent him to see Pastor Allen.

Allen talked with the man for a while, then took a pad of paper from his desk drawer. As he wrote, Allen said, "If you went to see a doctor, he would give you a prescription. So, that's what I'll do. Follow this prescription exactly as I write it. Five times a day for seven days I want you to read prayerfully and carefully the Twenty-third Psalm. When you awaken, before each meal, and at bedtime, read the psalm." The man agreed to do it. Allen says that in a week the man came back a different person.

If you haven't already, I hope that as you read this book, you will also memorize the Twenty-third Psalm. Read it prayerfully and carefully.

It will change your life.

Chapter 1

That's Enough

The LORD is my shepherd; I shall not want.

—Psalm 23:1

On Christmas Eve in 1875, David boarded a riverboat going up the Delaware River. David was sort of a minor celebrity. Over the past four or five years, he sang at several public events. Some of the passengers recognized him, and they insisted that he sing a song. David refused at first, but was finally persuaded. Since it was Christmastime, he thought about singing a Christmas carol, but a song had been stuck in his head all day. So, he decided to sing *Savior, Like a Shepherd Lead Us.*

When David finished singing, a man walked up and thanked him for his touching song. Then the man said, "I believe your Shepherd saved your life. ..."

Before I continue with David's story and what the stranger meant by, "I believe your Shepherd saved your life," I would like to introduce you to another David. David was the eighth and youngest son of Jesse. As a child, he worked as a shepherd in Bethlehem. One day, the prophet Samuel called him out of the field and anointed him to be the king of Israel. Several years would pass before he would rule on the throne, so young David simply returned to his sheep. Later, as king, David became known for his skills as a warrior and a writer of psalms.

David used the knowledge that he gained working as a shepherd to author perhaps one of the most beautiful compositions that has ever been written. Literary critics rate the Twenty-third Psalm as a masterpiece of lyric poetry. However, this wonderful psalm did not become one of the most beloved passages in the Word of God because of the praise of scholars. It is cherished for its universal theme of trust in God. Over the years of his life, David learned what it meant to trust in God.

Some believe David wrote the Twenty-third Psalm when he was a young shepherd during downtime in the fields. However, I don't think that was when he wrote it. There is too much in the psalm that gives the impression that David was a much older and more experienced man. Most Bible scholars believe David wrote the Twenty-third Psalm when he was in his fifties during a turbulent period in his kingdom. His son, Absalom, led a revolt, and many of his closest advisors betrayed him. David abandoned his palace in Jerusalem and fled for his life.

It was against that backdrop that David went back in his mind to his time as a shepherd boy and the precious time he spent with God. In what could now be described as the darkest and most painful time in his life, David wrote, *"The Lord is my shepherd; I shall not want."* Close your eyes for a moment and remember your most difficult challenge in

The Shepherd

life. Compare it with what David experienced. In the worst moment of your life, could you have said, *"The Lord is my shepherd; I shall not want?"*

The Person of the Shepherd

As we begin our look at David's masterpiece, I would like to point out three things about the first verse. First, I want to focus on the person of the Shepherd. Who is the Shepherd? David said, *"The LORD is my shepherd."* The word "LORD" is the personal name of God, YAHWEH. YAHWEH is my Shepherd.

Exodus chapter 3 is where we first find YAHWEH used. Moses was a shepherd tending to sheep when God appeared to him in a burning bush. God told him to go back to Egypt to bring the children of Israel out of slavery. Moses said to God, *"Behold, when I come unto the children of Israel, and shall say unto them, The God of your fathers hath sent me unto you; and they shall say to me, What is his name? what shall I say unto them?"* (Exodus 3:13). God answered and said, *"I Am That I Am."*

God's name is not a noun. God's name is a verb. It means a *continuous, unfinished action.* When God gave a name for His people to call Him, it expressed His dominion over all things, the source of His power, and His eternal nature: I AM. He is the self-sufficient, self-sustaining God who was, who is, and who will be. So, He tells Moses, "I AM."

The ancient Hebrew language that the Old Testament was written in did not have vowels in its alphabet. In written form, ancient Hebrew was a consonant-only language.

[20]

In the original Hebrew, God's name "I AM" transliterates to the letters *YHWH*. Bible scholars call these four letters the tetragrammaton, which means *four letters*. Over time, vowels were added to the four, which is where we get YAHWEH. In Jewish tradition, "YAHWEH is too sacred a name to utter out loud. Eventually, Jews started to substitute "Adonai," or "Elohim," for YAHWEH.

In the New Testament, in John 8, the Jews challenged the authority of Jesus. In doing so, they brought up Abraham. Jesus told them how glad Abraham was to see the day of the Lord. When the crowd asked how Jesus spoke as if He knew Abraham, Jesus answered, *"Verily, verily, I say unto you, Before Abraham was, I am"* (John 8:58). Jesus invoked the divine name of God for Himself. He said that He was "I AM."

Who is the Shepherd? Jesus said, *"I am the way, the truth, and the life: no man cometh unto the Father, but by me"* (John 14:6). Jesus is the Great I AM. He is the Great Shepherd.

Tony Evans tells the story of a man on a trip into the African rainforest. The man followed a guide. As they pushed onward into the deeper and darker jungle, the guide with his machete whacked away at the thick green growth that rose like a wall everywhere before them.

"How do you know where to go?" the man asked, "Where's the path?"

The guide replied, "I *am* the path."

It's a jungle out there, and we need a guide who knows where He's going and what He's doing. Jesus is that guide because He is the great I AM. He is the Great Shepherd who guides His sheep.

Years ago, when Saturday newspapers carried sermon

topics for the next day, Rev. R. I. Williams of Fairmont Park Methodist Church of Norfolk, Virginia, picked up the phone and called the newspaper to give them his sermon topic.

"The Lord is my Shepherd," he said.

The person on the other end said, "Is that all," and Reverend Williams said, "That's enough."

The next day the church page carried his sermon topic as, "The Lord is my Shepherd—That's Enough!"

The Lord is enough. That is the simple message of this first verse, and really of the entire psalm: If you make the Lord your Shepherd, you depend on Him to meet your needs. However, most of us today, are very independent. We don't like for people to have control over us. We don't like it when others make decisions for us. We like to be strong and in charge. Now it's okay if someone is dependent on us, but we don't want to be dependent on them.

A friend of mine saved and scrimped all his money. He saved and deposited in a bank account more money than he made in a year at his job. He called the account his "Take this job and shove it account." He told me that if his boss ever gets too bossy or if he doesn't treat him right, then he would quit. He is not dependent on his boss. He has a little money, so he can say, "Take this job and shove it."

Most of us are like my friend. We have issues with authority. We like our independence. We don't want anybody in authority over us. We want to make our own choices. However, when you say, "The Lord is my Shepherd," that means you depend on Him.

Remember David, who wrote the Twenty-third Psalm, was a shepherd. He knew what every shepherd knew. There are no such thing as a wild sheep. If sheep run away, they die. They cannot live in the wild. Sheep are domesticated. Sheep depend on the shepherd. Sheep depend on the shepherd for food. Sheep depend on the shepherd for direction. Sheep depend on the shepherd for protection from wild animals. Sheep depend on the shepherd for treatment from illness and disease. So, when you say someone else is your shepherd, you acknowledge that you need help. When you say that the Lord is your Shepherd, you recognize there is nobody better able to help you than God. You admit you are foolish, and God is wise. You confess you are ignorant, and God knows everything. You declare you are weak, and God is strong.

When you say, "the Lord is my Shepherd," you admit that God is trustworthy. You understand you can depend on Him. You realize that He has never, ever lost one of His sheep. You believe God is so dedicated to His flock that He would put His life on the line for one single lamb. That is why it is so wonderful to say, "The Lord is my Shepherd."

When David said, "The LORD is my shepherd," David said, "What I was to my father's sheep when I was a young man is what the Lord is to me." The good news is David's Shepherd from three thousand years ago is still our Shepherd today. You can count on the Lord. He will never leave you, nor forsake you.

The Possession of the Shepherd

So, first, this verse tells us something about the person of the Shepherd. Second, this verse tells us about the possession of the Shepherd. Notice that David says, *"The LORD is my Shepherd."* He does not say the Lord is *a* Shepherd. He says, "The LORD is *MY* shepherd." Sadly, today most of the world knows Jesus as *a* shepherd, but they don't know Him as *my* Shepherd. This passage is quoted by people everywhere, but it does not belong to everyone. This psalm only belongs to those who know the Lord as their Shepherd. The Twenty-third Psalm is not yours if you are not His.

When you say, "The LORD is *MY* shepherd," you admit ownership. A shepherd owns his sheep. In fact, a shepherd marks his sheep. Sometimes they brand the sheep, but that is not the best way. A brand is an identifying mark that is burned into the hide of livestock with a red-hot iron. Branding works great for cattle, but not for sheep. When the sheep's wool grows, it covers the brand, and the brand cannot be seen.

The modern way of marking sheep is to pierce the ear of the lamb and then attach an identification tag in the ear. The tags identify the owner of the sheep. However, that is a new way of marking sheep. For thousands of years, shepherds around the world notched sheep's ears. A shepherd always carried a very sharp knife to cut a piece out of the sheep's ear. Each shepherd used his own distinctive notch for the ear of his sheep. So, even if there were a large bunch of sheep gathered, the shepherd could easily identify his flock.

Branding, piercing, and cutting a notch out of an ear are painful ways to mark sheep. They are painful for the sheep and painful for the shepherd to inflict on the sheep he loves.

Similarly, if you are a Christian, you are owned by Jesus

Christ, and you are marked. Sometimes you are marked painfully through suffering and difficulty. It is painful to bear the mark of Jesus Christ, and it is also painful for Jesus to allow those marks to be burned, or pierced, or notched into your life.

Jesus said in Mark 8:34, *"Whosoever will come after me, let him deny himself, and take up his cross, and follow me."* Jesus said His sheep will bear crosses. We are not to take up Christ's cross, but we are to take up our own cross. There is a cross for you and a cross for me—that is, if we are going to follow Jesus. So, believers are marked by a cross, and the Lord can look at a crowd of people and easily identify His flock.

Remember, there are no such thing as wild sheep. If sheep run away, they die. Sheep cannot survive without a shepherd. Still, sheep are stubborn, and they often run anyway. There is a verse in the Old Testament written by the prophet Isaiah which says, *"All we like sheep have gone astray"* (Isaiah 53:6). Just like stubborn sheep, we are prone to wander away. All we like sheep have gone astray. We have all sinned. We have all went our own way instead of God's way. So, God sent His own Son out looking for us. He sent Jesus to get us back.

Imagine that there was a shepherd who had a lamb born to his flock. The shepherd notched the ear of the lamb that he owned, but the lamb ran away. The shepherd looked all over for the lamb. He searched and searched. After a long time, the shepherd did not find a baby lamb. Instead, he found a full-grown sheep for sale at a livestock auction. The shepherd recognized his mark in the sheep's ear. So, he went to the auctioneer and said, "That's my sheep. That's my mark." The auctioneer huffed, "Look buddy, you've got to bid and pay just like everybody else." So, the shepherd bids. The price kept going up because there was someone else bidding against him. Finally, the shepherd won, but he paid an outrageous price—way above reasonable market value. Still, he paid the price to get his lamb back. Now he has a double right to ownership.

That is what Jesus did for you. He has a right to own you because He created you. He also has a right to own you because He paid an outrageous price. He paid much, much more than you were worth. He paid with His own blood.

I recently spoke with a woman who said, "I grew up in church. I went to Sunday school. I learned John 3:16, but I didn't realize until I was an adult that I could have a personal relationship with Jesus Christ. It wasn't until I was grown, and somebody explained it to me that I understood." So, I want to be sure that you understand. Reading the Bible does not make you a Christian. Going to church does not make you a Christian. Putting money in the offering plate does not make you a Christian. Doing good works does not make you a Christian. To be a Christian is to choose Jesus Christ as Savior, Lord, and Shepherd. To be a Christian is a decision to become one of His sheep. To be a Christian is to have a personal relationship with Jesus Christ.

Once you say, "The Lord is **MY** Shepherd," and mean it, the Twenty-third Psalm becomes personal for you. Jesus reminded us of the personal relationship between shepherd and sheep when He said, "... *he calleth his own sheep by name*" (John 10:3). Does He know your name? Jesus further emphasized the personal relationship between the shepherd and sheep when He said, "... *the sheep follow him: for they know his voice*" (John 10:4). How close must sheep be to their shepherd? They must be close enough to hear his voice. Are you close enough to hear His voice? Can you say, "The Lord is *MY* Shepherd?"

Several years ago, a little nine-year-old boy named Donny suffered from leukemia. Donny's parents knew that he would die soon. So, they sent for their pastor, who came one night to visit Donny in the hospital. The disease had withered him away to skin and bones. Machines and tubes were hooked up to his frail little body. Donny was pale and very weak. He appeared to be only about half conscious and was unable to speak. The pastor was left alone in the hospital room with Donny. He sat with him, held his hand, and prayed. After some time, the pastor left the hospital, drove home, and went to bed.

Early the next morning, the pastor went back to the hospital to see Donny. He was too late. Donny died in the night. The pastor did his best to comfort Donny's parents. He prayed with them, and he grieved with them.

After a while, Donny's mother asked the pastor a question. She asked him if he knew any explanation for something strange that happened in the night. Donny's parents had never seen anything like it before. She said, "In the hours before Donny died, and up to the moment he died, he held with his right hand onto his fourth finger, the ring finger of his left hand. He died holding onto his finger.

The pastor began to weep. Through his tears, he shared with Donny's parents what he had said to their little boy the night before he died. He wanted to explain to that precious little child who was on the edge of eternity the importance of being a Christian in a way that he would understand. So, he took Donny's little hand. At first, he held his thumb and said, "The." He explained, "Donny, He is 'the' because He is one of a kind." Then he held his next finger and he said, "Lord—The Lord, God Himself." The pastor took Donny's third finger and said, "Is—He 'is' right here. He 'is' in this room right now with you, Donny." Then he took Donny's fourth finger and said, "My." The pastor told him about a personal commitment and relationship to Jesus Christ. Finally, he took his pinkie finger and said, "Shepherd—He is the 'Shepherd' who owns you, who died for you, who cares for you, and who loves you, Donny." The Lord is my Shepherd. The Lord is my Shepherd.

Even though Donny had not been able to speak a word, he heard. Before he died, he put his hand around his finger to say, "The Lord is **MY** Shepherd."

Is the Lord your Shepherd?

In Luke 15, Jesus told a story about a shepherd who counted his sheep. It was the custom of the ancient shepherds to count their sheep every evening. They knew exactly how many sheep they had, and even named each one. Jesus said that after the shepherd made his count, he noticed one missing. He counted ninety-nine and there should be one hundred. One lost sheep was out there somewhere without a shepherd. So the shepherd left the ninety and nine and traveled out into the wilderness. He looked until he found his sheep. Then, he picked up the sheep and carried him around his neck back to the safety of the sheepfold.

The point is: Jesus, like the shepherd, cares for one lost soul. If one person is reading this and doesn't know Christ as Lord and Savior, He is looking for you. And if you open your heart, Jesus will save you. Then you too can say, "The Lord is **MY** shepherd."

The Provision of the Shepherd

Psalm 23:1 tells us something about the person and the possession of the Shepherd. Thirdly, this verse tells us about the provision of the Shepherd. The meaning of *"I shall not want"* is "I will not lack." I heard a preacher put it this way, "Because the Lord is my Shepherd, I have everything I need."

In his book, *Praying the Twenty-third Psalm,* Elmer Towns recounted the story of a well-known minister who stood before a Sunday school gathering of small children and asked, "How many of you can quote Psalm 23?" Several of the children raised their hands, among them a beautiful little blonde-headed girl who could not have been much more than four years old. The pastor was surprised that such a young person would know Psalm 23. So, he asked her to come to the front of the room and recite it for the class.

Standing before the class with her hands clutched behind her back, the young girl smiled, and the pastor smiled back. Then, with great confidence, she said only this, "The Lord is my shepherd. That's all I want."

The little girl got the verse mixed up, but she got the message right. Understand that Psalm 23 is about your relationship with the Shepherd. When you get Him, everything else is secondary. "I shall not want" does not mean God is like a genie in a bottle who will fill your wish list. It is not about getting things from God. Now, it's okay to have things, but things are secondary. You must know why you have those things, who gave them to you, and how to use them properly. Also, be sure that your possessions never possess your heart. Let the Shepherd own your heart and fill your life.

The word that David used for "want" is the same word used in Deuteronomy to describe how God provided for His people. The Bible says, *"For the Lord thy God hath blessed thee in all the works of thy hand: he knoweth thy walking through this great wilderness: these forty years the Lord thy God hath been with thee; thou hast lacked nothing"* (Deuteronomy 2:7). The people of Israel wandered in the desert for forty years, but they did not lack anything. The Israelites were not sick in the wilderness. God kept them well. They were not hungry. God fed them with manna. They were not thirsty. God gave them water from the rock. For forty years, even their shoes did not wear out. They did not lack anything. It is the same idea. The Lord is my Shepherd; I will not lack or want.

David said with the Lord providing for you, then you will not lack what you need. You may have a different "want," but thank the Lord that He gives us what we need. This does not mean that there will not be times of drought, valleys, and needs (sometimes what we need is a valley experience). The remainder of this psalm shows that valley experiences do occur. However, the Great Shepherd will always know what we need and when to provide it.

Many years ago, a young woman brought home her fiancé to meet her parents. After dinner, her mother told her father to find out more about the young man. So, the girl's father invited the fiancé into his study. He said, "So, what are your plans?"

"I am a Bible scholar. I plan to be a pastor," he replied.

The father asked, "How do you plan to provide a house for my daughter?"

"I will study," the young man answered, "and God will provide."

"How will you pay for food?"

"God will provide."

"What about children? How will you support children?"

"God will provide."

The conversation continued for a while. Each time the father asked a question, the young man answered with, "God will provide." Later, the mother asked the father, "How did it go, honey?" The father frowned and said, "It's bad. He has no job and no plans." The mother said, "That's terrible." The father said, "It gets even worse. He thinks I'm God."

Now that's a funny story, but the truth is, no matter what inadequacy or hardship you are facing, no matter how problematic or distressful it may be—if the Lord is your Shepherd, He can provide. God can meet all your needs. It may not seem that way at times, but we must trust Him.

However, the only person who can say, "I shall not want" is the person who can say, "the Lord is *MY* shepherd." In life, there are two groups of people. You belong to one group or the other. Those in the first group are those who can say, *"The LORD is my shepherd; I shall not want."* Everyone else is in group two. They say "I am in want; therefore the Lord is not my shepherd." Is it really that simple? Yes. If there is emptiness and loneliness and frustration in your life, then at that point the Lord is not your Shepherd. If anyone or anything else besides the Lord shepherds you, you will not be satisfied. If your job shepherds you, you will be restless, unfulfilled, and frustrated. If education is your shepherd, you will be disillusioned. If drugs or alcohol are your shepherd, you will be wasted. If you depend on family or friends or church or possessions, you will be disappointed. Only when the Lord is your Shepherd will you be able to honestly say in your soul, *"I shall not want."*

I started this chapter with a story about a man named David who sang *Savior, Like a Shepherd Lead Us* on a riverboat on Christmas Eve in 1875. After David finished singing the hymn, a man came up to him and said, "I believe your Shepherd saved your life. Did you serve during the War?"

"Yes, sir. Yes, I did." David replied.

"Union?"

"Yes, sir, Union Army. I served from spring of 1860."

"Can you remember if you were doing picket duty on a bright moonlit night in 1862?"

"Well, yes, sir, I do recall such a night. Why do you ask?"

"I was there too, but I served in the Confederate Army. When I saw you standing at your post, I said to myself, 'That fellow will never get away from here alive.' I raised my musket and took aim. I stood in the shadow completely concealed, while the full light of the moon fell upon you."

"Why didn't you shoot?"

"At that instant, you raised your eyes to heaven and began to sing the same song. Music, especially song, has always had a wonderful power over me, and I took my finger off the trigger. 'Let him sing his song to the end,' I said to myself. 'I can shoot him afterwards.' But the song you sang then was the song you sang just now. As you sang, you reached the place where it says, *'We are Thine, do Thou befriend us, Be the guardian of our way …'* I could hear every word perfectly, and how the memories came to my heart. I began to think of my childhood and my God-fearing mother. She had many, many times sung that song to me. But she died all too soon, otherwise much in my life would no doubt have been different."

"I am sorry for your loss, but why didn't you shoot?"

"When you had finished your song, it was impossible for me to take aim at you again, though you still stood in the bright moonlight, a perfect target. I thought, 'The Lord who is able to save that man from certain death must surely be great and mighty,' and my arm of its own accord dropped limp at my side. I cannot tell you all the things I thought at that time. My heart was smitten, but I didn't know what to do. Just now, when you were about to sing and stood quietly as if praying, I recognized you. I've wandered far and wide since that other occasion. I have never found that Shepherd. Please help me now find a cure for my sick soul."

David was deeply moved and threw his arms about the man who had been his enemy, who, indeed, could have ended his life. That Christmas Eve night, a former soldier found the great and tender Shepherd as his Savior.

David went on to become a very famous American Gospel singer and composer. You probably will remember him by his full name: Ira David Sankey. Sankey became well-known as the music minister for Dwight L. Moody. He pioneered a musical style that influenced church services and evangelical campaigns for generations. Ira D. Sankey composed over a thousand hymns, most of which continue to be sung today.

Today, the world has the musical legacy of Ira D. Sankey because on a moonlit evening in 1862 he sang, *"Savior, like a shepherd lead us, much we need Thy tender care; In Thy pleasant pastures feed us, for our use Thy folds prepare."*

The Lord is truly a Good Shepherd to His sheep.

Are you in His flock?

Savior, Like a Shepherd Lead Us
by Dorothy A. Thrupp

Savior, like a shepherd lead us,
Much we need Thy tender care;
In Thy pleasant pastures feed us,
For our use Thy folds prepare:
Blessed Jesus, blessed Jesus,
Thou hast bought us, Thine we are;
Blessed Jesus, blessed Jesus,
Thou hast bought us, Thine we are.

We are Thine, do Thou befriend us,
Be the guardian of our way;
Keep Thy flock, from sin defend us,
Seek us when we go astray:
Blessed Jesus, blessed Jesus,
Hear, O hear us when we pray;
Blessed Jesus, blessed Jesus,
Hear, O hear us when we pray.

Thou hast promised to receive us,
Poor and sinful though we be;
Thou hast mercy to relieve us,
Grace to cleanse, and pow'r to free:
Blessed Jesus, blessed Jesus,
Early let us turn to Thee;
Blessed Jesus, blessed Jesus,
Early let us turn to Thee.

Early let us seek Thy favor,
Early let us do Thy will;
Blessed Lord and only Savior,
With Thy love our bosoms fill:
Blessed Jesus, blessed Jesus,
Thou hast loved us, love us still;
Blessed Jesus, blessed Jesus,
Thou hast loved us, love us still.

Chapter 2

The Right Path

> *He maketh me to lie down in green pastures:*
> *he leadeth me beside the still waters.*
> *He restoreth my soul:*
> *he leadeth me in the paths of righteousness for his name's sake.*
>
> – Psalm 23:2–3

Many years ago, a young U.S. Navy ensign, after nearly completing his first overseas cruise, was given an opportunity to display his capabilities at getting the ship underway. He barked out commands, and men ran all around the ship carrying out his orders. Soon the ship headed out of the channel on its way back to United States. The ensign felt proud. His efficiency, in fact, established a new record for getting a destroyer underway, so he was not surprised when a seaman approached with a message from the captain. He was a bit surprised, however, to find it was a radio message and even more surprised to read, "My personal congratulations upon completing your underway preparation exercise according to the book and with amazing speed. In your haste, however, you have overlooked one of the unwritten rules—make sure the captain is aboard the ship before getting underway."

Have you ever gotten in such a hurry to take off on some part of your journey through life and you didn't make sure that Jesus was on board? That question is appropriate since the Twenty-third Psalm is about a lifelong journey. We, just like sheep, sometimes do not know where we are going or how to get there. That is why we need a Shepherd to guide us on the right path.

David used the imagery of the shepherd guiding his sheep on the right path when he composed the Twenty-third Psalm. It's amazing to think that three thousand years have gone by since David wrote these words. The throne from which King David reigned, the harp that he played, and his copy of the Book of the Law on which he meditated day and night are all buried under the debris of history. However, the Twenty-third Psalm is as fresh and relevant today as it was in the hour it was first written. We still need a Shepherd to guide us on the right path.

The Shepherd Provides Rest

As the Good Shepherd guides, He also provides. There are three benefits that our Shepherd provides. First, the Shepherd provides rest. Psalm 23:2 reads, *"He maketh me to lie down in green pastures: he leadeth me beside the still waters."* This verse speaks of rest. Throughout the remainder of this psalm, the sheep move. However, they start here with rest. This is a great principle in the spiritual life. You must stop before you start. You need to stop and rest before you can do anything successfully for the Lord.

God wants you to stop. I am sure you have a lot of busy stuff to do, but is there anything as important as your walk with God? Don't you think that if you spend some quality time with God and get yourself restored, rejuvenated, and revived, you're going to be better at everything else you're doing?

Our lives are filled with business, concerns, and stress. Often, we don't rest easily. We are restless, but we need rest. It is important to have a daily quiet time with God. Jesus said, *"Come unto me, all ye that labour and are heavy laden, and I will give you rest. Take my yoke upon you, and learn of me; for I am meek and lowly in heart: and ye shall find rest unto your souls"* (Matthew 11:28–29). The Christian life starts with rest.

The Shepherd Ministers

The Shepherd ministers to His sheep. Notice the first part of Psalm 23:2, *"He maketh me to lie down in green pastures."* Did you know sheep will not lie down unless all their needs are met? If sheep are hungry, thirsty, troubled, or afraid, they will not lie down. Everything must be just right for sheep to rest.

In ancient Israel, the shepherds took their sheep out into the pasture around 4 a.m. each morning. The sheep grazed until sometime between 10 a.m. to noon when it got too hot. Then the shepherd found a shaded place where the sheep could lie down and rest. All morning long, the shepherd provided for the needs of the sheep so they could rest in the hot afternoon.

David wrote in Psalm 23:2–3 that the shepherd "leads."

He doesn't drive the sheep. Why? When a shepherd used his staff to drive his sheep in a particular direction, they scattered in all directions. They ran astray. The prophet Isaiah knew something about sheep when he wrote, *"All we like sheep have gone astray"* (Isaiah 53:6a). Isaiah used sheep to describe all of us because like sheep we tend to go astray.

"All we like sheep have gone astray" speaks of aimless wandering—of a restless life. That may be your life. Are you wandering aimlessly without a purpose? Is that why all your relationships have failed? Is that why you are miserable at your job? Is that why money doesn't satisfy you? Is that why the bottle doesn't help you? Is that why those pills leave you empty inside? You don't have to continue to wander aimlessly. Once you know Jesus, you will finally have satisfaction. You will have rest.

The mere presence of the shepherd puts the sheep at peace. When he is near, they don't panic, and they don't fight. They can lay down in peaceful slumber. It's the same with you and me. Nothing reduces stress like the presence of the Shepherd. When you are living in close connection to Jesus, you can sleep, you can relax, you can rest.

One of the primary needs of sheep is water. An average healthy sheep needs several gallons of water per day. Multiply that by the size of the herd and you understand that shepherds were always on the lookout for water. David used the picture of the shepherd searching for water when he wrote, *"he leadeth me beside the still waters."*

I attended the University of Oklahoma. One of my best friends went to Oklahoma State University. Oklahoma and Oklahoma State have a friendly in-state rivalry. So, my friend and I always joke and kid with each other whenever the Sooners play the Cowboys. One year, before the Bedlam football game, my friend called and said, "God is for OSU." I said, "You are out of your mind. God doesn't take sides in football." He said, "Oh, yeah. Well, the Bible says that God leads me beside 'Stillwater!'" It's sort of funny when you understand the campus of Oklahoma State is in Stillwater, Oklahoma.

The real meaning of "still waters" has to do with sheep needing still, quiet waters to drink. They cannot be watered at a place where the water is swift. Sheep are deathly afraid of rushing water. Even if they are thirsty, they will not drink from a rushing stream or river. So, the shepherd must find a calm pool to water the sheep.

If you are a Christian, your Shepherd provides still waters for you. When your life seems like a rampaging river, the Lord comes and stills the water. Jesus said, *"Peace I leave with you, my peace I give unto you: not as the world giveth, give I unto you. Let not your heart be troubled, neither let it be afraid"* (John 14:27). When the storms of life rage, you can count on Jesus to calm the gale and give you peace. The Shepherd provides green pastures and still waters so His sheep can rest.

The Shepherd Makes ...

The Shepherd "makes" His sheep lie down in green pastures. Sometimes, sheep were restless, even with everything provided for them. Sometimes, they would not lie down. So, the shepherd gently placed his hand on the back of the sheep and pushed to "make" them lie down. The shepherd knew that rest was essential, so he "makes" them lie down.

When my daughter, Abby, was very little, she used to fight going to sleep. Each night, we battled. She acted tired and fussy, but she refused to go to sleep. She said, "I don't want to go night-night." So, I picked her up and put her head on my shoulder and started to pat her back. She knew that once she laid her head down, she would be overcome by drowsiness and fall asleep. So, she leaned her head back away from my shoulder, and I gently pushed her back down. Eventually, as I patted her back, she gave out and fell asleep.

Sometimes, the Lord must give us a push to lie down. We need rest, and if you do not rest willingly, God may allow trials and struggles to come into your life to make you lie down. Your "green pasture" might be a white-sheeted hospital bed. God knows that you need rest.

God is compelling you to rest. If He must, He will make you rest. God looks at His sheep when they wander off and He says, "You need to stop whatever it is you're doing. You need to lie down in these green pastures. You need to rest."

The Shepherd Provides Restoration

In addition to rest, the Shepherd provides restoration. That is the meaning of *"He restoreth my soul."* The word, "restore" means *to make new*. When I was a young man, I bought a used, dented, rusty 1965 Ford Mustang. The car ran all right, but it looked terrible. I worked, scrimped, and saved to come up with enough money to restore the old car. When I finished the body work and applied new paint, the Mustang looked new. When I ran my hand over the surface of the car body, it felt as good as new. When the Lord restores your soul, you are like new. You have a new start or a new beginning.

Downcast Sheep Need Restoration

There are two types of sheep that need restoration. The first are called "downcast sheep." This comes from an old English shepherd's term, "cast," which describes a sheep that has turned over on its back and cannot get up by itself. All a "cast" sheep can do is lay on its back with its legs in the air, frantically kicking to get up, without success. Sheep have a four-chambered stomach. If they are not turned upright, gases build up which will cause death. If they are not turned upright, blood circulation will be cut off from the legs which will eventually kill the sheep. If they are not turned upright, wolves will have an easy meal of mutton. If the shepherd does not arrive within a reasonably short time, the downcast sheep will die.

I don't know about you, but there have been times in my life when I have found myself spiritually on my back. I needed Someone to put me back on my feet. I was totally helpless, and I needed my Shepherd to restore me.

Are you downcast? Is your world turned upside down? Jesus can restore your soul. You have a Shepherd that loves you. He can get you right-side-up and back on your feet again.

Disobedient Sheep Need Restoration

The shepherd doesn't only restore downcast sheep, he also restores disobedient sheep. Remember, it is not unusual for sheep to wander away from the flock. The same is true of us. We are prone to wander.

Several years ago, in a little country schoolhouse, a fourth-grade teacher asked her students, "If you have one hundred sheep in a pen and one wanders through a hole in the fence, how many sheep would be left?"

A little girl raised her hand and answered, "Ninety-nine."

The teacher said, "That's correct, Brenda." However, before she could continue with the lesson a little boy in the back of the class raised his hand. "Yes, Tommy," the teacher said.

"Teacher," Tommy exclaimed, "that answer is wrong. The answer is zero. There would be no sheep left."

The teacher smiled and said, "No, young man. One hundred minus one is ninety-nine. You just don't understand arithmetic."

Tommy said, "Ma'am, you don't understand sheep. I live on a farm, and if one gets out, they all get out."

Sheep are prone to wander. Sheep easily become over-confident, rebellious, or distracted, and they wander away. They see greener grass in the other direction and take off. They move further and further away from the shepherd.

Once, a man took a job with a government subcontractor to paint the white lines down the center of the highway. His foreman ordered him to paint the lines by hand and the man went to work.

After three days, the foreman said, "I'm afraid that I'm going to have to let you go."

"Why?" the man asked.

"Your performance has dropped. On your first day, you did great. You painted the line for three miles. Your second day wasn't bad either. You painted two miles. But today you only painted one mile. So, I'm going to have to fire you. I'm sorry."

On his way out of the office, the fired employee looked back and said, "It's not my fault. Every day I got further away from the paint can."

We can be like that sometimes. Do you ever feel like you are moving further and further away from the Lord? When that happens, the Lord seeks you out to restore you. Remember, shepherds in ancient Israel counted their sheep each night one by one. If the shepherd found one missing, he secured the other sheep in the sheepfold and set off looking for the lost sheep. When the shepherd found the sheep, he carried him back to the safety of the sheepfold. That is the picture Jesus gave of Himself in Luke 15:4–6. He is the Good Shepherd seeking His lost sheep.

But sometimes, straying sheep become stubborn sheep. Sometimes, one sheep continued to wander off each day. If that sheep persisted to wander, he would likely get eaten by a wolf. So, the shepherd took drastic action. He broke one of the sheep's legs. Then the shepherd bound up the leg in a splint. The sheep became dependent on the shepherd to pick him up and help him over difficult places. The shepherd carried the helpless sheep close to his heart. When the sheep finally healed, he stayed closer to the shepherd than any of the other sheep. The shepherd broke the sheep's leg, not to hurt it, but to restore it.

David wrote the Twenty-third Psalm later in life while on the run from his son, Absalom. When David wrote of restoration, he probably remembered back to his adulterous affair with Bathsheba. The story is told in 2 Samuel 11–12.

Years earlier, King David chose to stay home in Jerusalem while he sent the rest of the Israelite army to fight other nations and kings. While David relaxed and walked on the palace roof, he saw a beautiful woman bathing on her roof. David was sexually attracted to the woman. So, he sent messengers to discern her identity. The messengers returned and told David that her name was Bathsheba, the wife of Uriah. Despite knowing she was married, David sent for her, and they committed adultery. Later, Bathsheba sent word to David that she was pregnant with his child.

David was nervous that his sin would now be found out. He called for Uriah to come home so that he could spend a night with his wife and cover up the sin that Bathsheba was pregnant. However, Uriah refused to sleep with his wife while his fellow men were off fighting. So, David sent Uriah back to war. Uriah carried a note from the king to the army commander. The note contained instructions to put Uriah at the frontline and withdraw, which resulted in Uriah's death. Bathsheba mourned her husband. Then she moved to the palace and married King David.

Sometime later, the prophet Nathan visited King David. Nathan shared a story about a lamb:

> There were two men in one city; the one rich, and the other poor. The rich man had exceeding many flocks and herds: But the poor man had nothing, save one little ewe lamb, which he had bought and nourished up: and it grew up together with him, and with his children; it did eat of his own meat, and drank of his own cup, and lay in his bosom, and was unto him as a daughter. And there came a traveller unto the rich man, and he spared to take of his own flock and of his own herd, to dress for the wayfaring

man that was come unto him; but took the poor man's lamb, and dressed it for the man that was come to him.

—2 Samuel 12:1b-4

When David heard Nathan's story, he was outraged. He said, "The man that did this thing will surely die." The prophet looked at the king and said, *"Thou art the man"* (2 Samuel 12:7). David was heartbroken when he realized that he was the rich man, Uriah was the poor man, and Bathsheba was the sheep in Nathan's story. So, he poured out his soul to God by writing Psalm 51. In poetic style, David begged God for restoration. He wrote, *"Restore unto me the joy of thy salvation; and uphold me with thy free spirit"* (Psalm 51:12).

David repented, and God restored him, but I believe God also crippled David. There were consequences to David's actions. God said to David, *"The sword shall never depart from thine house"* (2 Samuel 12:10). God broke David's leg and for the rest of his life, he walked with a limp. The first child he bore with Bathsheba died. Several of his sons rebelled against him. His son Absalom took his throne, which forced David to flee into exile. David's family fell apart. God forgave David, but the forgiveness did not wipe out the consequences of David's sin.

David was, in the words of the Bible, a man after God's own heart. He also was a man subject to weakness. Every Christian can identify with David. We want to be men and women after God's own heart, and we also know what it means to fall. Still, like David, we too can experience God's grace, mercy, and strength in our lives everyday

The Lord restored David. He will restore you too—no matter what you have done. Even when you are a stubborn, straying sheep, the Good Shepherd will seek you and bring you back. No matter how far you have strayed, Jesus will restore you.

The Shepherd Provides Right Paths

So, first, the Shepherd provides rest. Second, the Shepherd provides restoration. Thirdly, the Shepherd provides right paths. The Bible says, *"He leadeth me in the paths of righteousness for his name's sake"* (Psalm 23:3b). When you stray into the path of unrighteousness, the Good Shepherd can put you back on the right path.

What is the right path? The right path is the path that follows the Shepherd. Jesus said, *"My sheep hear my voice, and I know them, and they follow me"* (John 10:27). Be careful who you follow in this life. Get on the right path and follow Jesus.

In the dashboard of my truck, there is a built in Garmin Navigator—a GPS. I have come to appreciate the simplicity of my GPS. All I do is type in an address and a voice talks to me telling me where to go. It's a woman's voice. Before, I had a GPS, there was a woman—my wife—sitting on the passenger side who told me where to go. So, I was happy with a woman's voice. I named the GPS voice "Betty." Because I drive a Ford, the voice is Betty Ford. Some of you are too young to remember Betty Ford. If you ask your grandparents, they will tell you about Betty Ford, and you will get the joke.

One day, Betty said, "Caution," as I drove on the interstate with nothing around me. I looked around for what I should caution. She said it again, "Caution." I looked down at the speedometer. I was speeding—seventy miles per hour in a sixty mile-per-hour zone. I don't know how in the world Betty knew that I drove that fast, but she said it again, "Caution." I drove about fifteen miles trying to figure out how she knew my speed. Was she watching? Is there a satellite in the sky? The GPS knew that I was speeding, so she said, "Caution."

Sometimes, when I miss a road that I'm supposed to turn on, Betty gets mad. She gets this huff in her voice. She says, "Huff—recalculating—recalculating route." Then she says, "Make a U-turn. Turn around." She has this attitude like she is saying to me, "Hey stupid, you missed your road. It's right back there. You're going the wrong way. Turn around."

If you have a GPS and you take the wrong route, the GPS recalculates and gives you an alternative route. Even though you were disobedient to the first route; even though you rebelled and chose your own route, the GPS adjusts to your stubbornness and gets you back on the right route.

If you are a believer in Jesus Christ, then you have Someone living inside of you called the Holy Spirit. The Holy Spirit tells you, "Caution," whenever you drift off into sin. The still small voice inside of you says, "Make a U-turn. Change your direction. Turn around. Confess your sin and get back on the right path to God." The Bible calls that grace. Grace is where God meets you even when you've messed up. God meets you where you failed, creates an alternate route, and brings you home.

Why does God put you back on the right path? The Bible says it is *"for his name's sake."* God wants to keep His own reputation as a Good Shepherd. The character and reputation of the Shepherd are bound up in the lives and the health of His sheep. The shepherd knows the best way to get the sheep to their destination safely. Shepherds stake their reputation on their ability to not lose a sheep along the way. Our shepherd is guiding us along the path that is best for us for His name's sake—His reputation is tied to it.

Many years ago, a young pastor visited an elderly, dying woman. During their conversation, the woman told the pastor she positively knew she would go to Heaven when she died because she knew the Lord. In fact, she said she was looking forward to death because she knew she would go be with Jesus. The young pastor thought it sounded arrogant and overconfident for her to say those kinds of things. He asked, "Are you sure about that?" She replied, "If I'm not in Heaven, the Good Lord will lose more than I lose. All that I can lose is my soul because that's all I have. But if I should not end up in Heaven, the Lord would lose His reputation. For He has promised to save all who trust Jesus."

The Good Shepherd will provide rest, restoration, and right paths. He won't fail you because His reputation is at stake. Everything He does, He does for His name's sake.

Chapter 3
Through the Valley

> *Yea, though I walk through the valley of the shadow of death, I will fear no evil: for thou art with me; thy rod and thy staff they comfort me.*
>
> —Psalm 23:4

A preacher began his sermon by glaring out over the congregation and proclaiming in a very loud voice, "Every member of this church is going to die." Most of the congregation looked somber at this, and he started to proceed when he noticed one man in the front row who smiled back at him. So, he decided to say it again, more loudly this time. "I said every member of this church is going to die!" For emphasis, he hit his fist on the pulpit. Well, the rest of the congregation looked even more grim, but the man in the front row still just smiled at him. The preacher was frustrated at this, so he mustered up all his energy and with as much volume and drama as he could summon, he said a third time, "I said every member of this church is going to die!" The man in the front row smiled even wider. At this point the preacher called him out. "You there, did you hear what I said?" The man answered, "Yes sir, you said that every member of this church is going to die." So, the preacher asked him, "Then why are you smiling?" And the man replied: "Because I'm not a member of this church!"

That's a funny story, but the truth is death is not something we like to talk about. However, it is something we all must face. They say there are two things that are inevitable—death and taxes. I am sure everyone reading this has paid taxes. I am also sure you have experienced the death of a relative or a close friend. Death is very common, yet we rarely talk about it. We are uncomfortable talking about it.

Even though we don't like to talk about death, we like to talk about this psalm. In the forward of this book, I wrote that I believe that Psalm 23 is the best-known chapter in the Bible. I also believe that Psalm 23:4 is the best-known, most quoted verse in this chapter. Chances are, if you attend a Christian or Jewish funeral, this verse will be read. It touches us in times of grief and sorrow. For three thousand years, people have turned to these words in their time of greatest need for comfort and hope.

On September 11, 2001, our country was attacked. Al-Qaeda terrorists carried out four coordinated attacks resulting in 2,977 deaths and over 25,000 injuries. It was the deadliest terrorist attack in human history. That night, President George W. Bush delivered a brief message from the White House to comfort and reassure the nation. Of all the passages in the Bible he could have quoted, President Bush quoted Psalm 23:4:

Tonight, I ask for your prayers for all those who grieve, for the

children whose worlds have been shattered, for all whose sense of safety and security has been threatened. And I pray they will be comforted by a power greater than any of us spoken through the ages in Psalm 23: "Even though I walk through the valley of the shadow of death, I fear no evil, for You are with me."
—President George H.W. Bush, September 11, 2001

The Picture of the Valley

Psalm 23:4 is beloved because it speaks of hope in the dark days of life. Life is not always filled with green pastures and still waters. Life also has dark valleys. The valley of the shadow of death could represent any dark moment in life, but it certainly emphasizes the darkest moment of all—the passing from life unto death. Death is the final valley.

There are three things that I would like to point out about the valley. First, notice the picture of the valley. David understood what it meant to travel through valleys, and he used them as a poetic way to describe the dark valleys that we all go through in life. With his words, David remembered back to his time as a shepherd boy and painted a picture of the valley.

The hill country of Judah where David grew up and shepherded sheep is broken up by many deep valleys known as *wadis*. A wadi is a ravine that is dry except during the rainy season. Wadis were very dangerous places. They were infested with predators. Criminals used the wadis as hideouts. Storms quickly flooded the wadis—a problem that continues in the region today. According to a *Jerusalem Post* article dated April 27, 2018, ten Israeli teenagers were killed when they were swept away by a flash flood during a hike through a wadi at Nahal Tsafit, south of the Dead Sea. The wadi valleys in Israel were and still are extremely dangerous.

When the spring arrived, the shepherds in ancient Israel headed for higher ground for the summer. The shepherd knew the scorching sun would soon burn up all the grass. So, he moved his flock to the hills where there would be plenty of grasslands, fresh water, and cooler temperatures. The snow from the mountaintops melted, revealing fresh fields of grass. As the shepherd led his sheep to higher ground, he traveled through many valleys.

The sheep now experienced the most challenging part of their journey as they followed their shepherd through the dark valleys. Danger lurked in the dark places. This was the season of the year when sheep learn to stay as close to their shepherd as possible. Their life depended on it.

David led his sheep through valleys to mountaintops on numerous occasions. The Bible alludes to one of those occasions in 1 Samuel 16. The prophet Samuel searched for a new king to anoint. After he passed over David's older seven brothers, Samuel waited for David to return from tending the sheep. If the sheep were home, no waiting would have been involved. Therefore, the assumption is that David took the herd to the mountains, but returned at Samuel's request and was subsequently anointed as king of Israel. After being anointed, he went back to the field to tend to his flock (1 Samuel 16:4–13).

David knew the valley well. He was especially acquainted with the valley of the shadow of death. He faced that valley many times. He faced death when he stood against the giant warrior, Goliath. He faced death as he fought Philistine armies. He faced death from the fury of King Saul. Even as he wrote this psalm, he faced death from his own son, Absalom. David stared death in the face many times and he lived to write about it.

Perhaps, like David, you too are familiar with this valley. If not, someday, you will be introduced. Unless the Lord returns in our lifetime, you and I must walk through the valley of the shadow of death. Three people die every second. Eleven thousand people die every hour. Two hundred and fifty thousand people die every day. Statistics say that ten out of ten people die. If the Lord tarries, you, and I will die. Death is inevitable no matter how you try to avoid it.

On July 5, 2002, Ted Williams, the famous Major League Baseball player, was cryogenically frozen. His son, John-Henry Williams, believed that his father could be preserved at the time of his death and brought back in the future. However, the process of cryonics can only begin after clinical death. People who are cryogenically frozen are legally dead. So, Ted Williams is a frozen corpse. His death was unavoidable.

Perhaps one of most well-known examples of a person who tried to avoid death was Sarah Winchester. Sarah was the widow of William Winchester and heiress to the fortune he made from the sale of Winchester firearms. As the story goes, a medium told Sarah that if her home in San Jose, California, remained unfinished, she would never die. So, she started the world's longest home renovation project. Sarah hired construction teams to work around the clock. From 1886 to 1922 construction never stopped as the original eight-room farmhouse grew into the world's most unusual and sprawling mansion. Today, the Winchester

House has over 24,000 square feet of living space, and contains 160 rooms, 10,000 windows, 2,000 doors, 47 fireplaces, and 13 bathrooms. However, construction on the mansion ended on September 2, 1922, when Sarah Winchester died. No matter how hard she tried, death was unavoidable.

Yes, death is unavoidable. You can't escape it. Death casts a long shadow over every person. However, if you are a Christian, all you face is the shadow of death.

Donald Grey Barnhouse, who was a pastor at Tenth Presbyterian Church in Philadelphia for many years, lost his wife when his daughter was still a child. Dr. Barnhouse tried to help his little girl process the death of her mother. Once, as they drove, a huge moving van passed them. As it passed, the shadow of the truck swept over the car. Barnhouse had a thought. He said, "Would you rather be run over by a truck, or by its shadow?"

His daughter replied, "By the shadow, of course. That can't hurt us at all."

Dr. Barnhouse replied, "Right. If the truck doesn't hit you, but only its shadow, then you are fine. Well, it was only the shadow of death that went over your mother. She's actually alive—more alive than we are. And that's because two thousand years ago, the real truck of death hit Jesus. And because death crushed Jesus, and we believe in Him, now the only thing that can come over us is the shadow of death, and the shadow of death is but the entrance into glory."

Shadows can't hurt you. That's why David calls it *"the valley of the shadow of death."* The shadow fell on Jesus and He defeated death. Jesus took the sting out of sin, and the dread out of the grave. When the shadow passes over, you go immediately into the presence of the Lord. The believer in Christ has this assurance: beyond the shadow of death is the sunlight of the eternal morning.

Shadows do not exist unless there is a light somewhere. If you are a Christian, the light of Jesus will never disappear from your life. Don't look at the shadow. Look instead at the light, and the shadow will fall behind you.

The Presence in the Valley

So, first we see a picture of the valley. Second, there is a presence in the valley. What is the problem that most people have when it comes to death? It is fear. Yet, David wrote, "I will fear no evil." Why should we fear no evil? Because "thou art with me." If you are a believer, there is a presence in the valley with you.

The Person with You

When you walk through the valley of the shadow of death, you have nothing to fear because of the Person with you. Just like the shepherd led his sheep through the valley, the Good Shepherd leads you through the dark valleys of your life.

A little boy was afraid of the dark. One night his mother told him to go out to the back porch and bring her the broom. The little boy turned to his mother and said, "Mama, I don't want to go out there. It's dark."

His mother smiled reassuringly at her son. "You don't have to be afraid of the dark," she explained. "Jesus is out there. He'll look after you and protect you."

The little boy looked at his mother with a confused

stare and asked, "Are you sure he's out there?"

"Yes, I'm sure. He is everywhere, and He is always ready to help you when you need him," she said.

The little boy thought about that for a minute. Then he went to the back door and cracked it open a little. Peering out into the darkness, he yelled, "Jesus? If you're out there, would you please hand me the broom?"

Understand that Jesus is with you in the darkness of life and in the darkness of death. If you are a believer, Jesus is with you always. He will never leave you, nor forsake you. That means Jesus will never leave you in life, and He will never leave you in death.

Did you notice there is a change in pronouns in Psalm 23:4. David had used the pronoun "he" to represent the Lord in the previous verses. In this verse, he changed to the pronoun "you." In the first three verses of the Twenty-third Psalm, David talked *about* the Shepherd, but here he talks *to* the Shepherd. It became personal for David.

A mother and her small son traveled from Chicago to California by train. Like all small boys, the child became restless. He got up from his seat, went to the end of the car, and got a drink of water. He came back to his seat, and a few moments later, he ran down to the end of the passenger car again. After this happened several times, a woman sitting across the aisle felt sorry for the little boy's mother. She called the youngster over and said, "That is a lovely suit you have on."

The little boy smiled with pride. He said, "My mommy made it. She cut out the material and stitched it together. She sewed on these buttons. She even put a buckle on my pants."

As he told the woman what his mother had done, the train plunged into a tunnel. Darkness blanketed the locomotive. The little boy left the woman and ran across the aisle. He threw his arms around his mother's legs and said, "Mommy, Mommy, you're here and I'm not scared, am I?"

It was one thing to talk about his mother while the train was in the sunshine. But in the darkness, the little boy no longer talked about his mother. He talked to her. David, like the little boy on the train, did the same thing. While he thought about rest, refreshment, and lush green pastures, he talked about the Shepherd. But when he thought about the dark valleys in his life, and the darkest valley through which he was sure to go, he spoke to God directly. He talked to the Person with him.

The Power with You

Not only do you have nothing to fear because of the Person with you, you have nothing to fear because of the power with you. David wrote, *"… thy rod and thy staff they comfort me."* The rod and the staff were the main implements the shepherd used to defend and protect his flock. They symbolized his power.

The rod was used to defend the sheep against attacking wild animals. It was a wooden club about two feet long with a round head into which the shepherd pounded sharp pieces of stone or metal. A skilled shepherd used the rod as a weapon to smash the skull of an attacking predator.

David, as a shepherd, illustrated the use of the rod before he went out to defeat Goliath. He told Saul of the time he killed a lion and a bear to rescue his sheep. It seemed that David used a rod to kill the lion and bear. When Goliath saw him, the giant cursed David and said, *"Am I a dog, that thou comest to me with staves?"* (1 Samuel 17:43). The word "staves" means *rods*.

The staff functioned differently. Whereas the rod was used for defense, the staff was used for control. The staff was also known as a shepherd's crook. Usually, the staff was about six feet long. Shepherds used the crook at the end of the staff to rescue sheep which fell into a cleft or crevasse and to control the flock. Just as the sheep took comfort from the shepherd's power, you can take comfort knowing the Lord will guide and protect you from harm, even when you walk through a dark valley.

The early Native Americans had a unique practice of training young braves. On the night of a boy's thirteenth birthday, after learning hunting, scouting, and fishing skills, he was put to one final test. He journeyed to a dense forest to spend the entire night alone. Until then, he had never been away from the security of the family and the tribe. But on that night, he was blindfolded and taken several miles away. When he removed the blindfold, he was in the middle of a thick woods. The night alone was terrifying. Every time a twig snapped; he visualized a wild animal ready to pounce. After what seemed like an eternity, dawn broke and the first rays of sunlight entered the interior of the forest. Looking around, the boy saw flowers, trees, and the outline of the path. Then, to his utter astonishment, he beheld the figure of a man standing just a few feet away, armed with a bow and arrow. It was his father. He had been there all night long.

If you are a Christian, your heavenly Father is watching over you even in your darkest night. You find protection, not in the absence of danger, but in the power of God. When you had that close call, it was the hand of God. When something stopped you suddenly, keeping you out of harm's way, it was the power of the Lord.

The Path Through the Valley

So, we have seen the picture of the valley, and the presence in the valley. Thirdly, notice the path through the valley. There is one word in Psalm 23:4 that captures my attention. That is the word *through*. There is no way around the dark valleys of life. We all must go through them. However, the psalm doesn't say this valley is where the path ends. It is not a cave with a dead end. You start at one end of the valley and you come out the other side. You go *through* the valley. The Shepherd leads you to the valley and he leads you *through* the valley.

Christian singer and comedian Mark Lowry was once asked about his favorite Scripture verse. He said, "My life verse is this: 'And it came to pass.' I love that verse, don't you? 'And it came to pass.' It didn't come to stay. It came to pass. No matter what you are going through, it will pass, or you will pass. No matter what you are going through, this too shall pass."

Right now, you are either entering a valley, going through a valley, or coming out of a valley. Wherever you are on your path of life, this too shall pass. As you travel your path, take comfort in knowing that God is with you. Sometimes, it may seem like the journey to the top takes forever. Just keep your eye on the Shepherd and look up where He leads you. You will get there. You will get through your valley.

The preacher looked at me when I was eleven years old and he read, *"Yea, though I walk through the valley of the shadow of death, I will fear no evil: for thou art with me; thy rod and thy staff they comfort me."* That moment stands out in my mind still today. It was my mother's funeral. I memorized the Twenty-third Psalm in Sunday school. I knew the words, but in that moment, they became personal to me.

Over the years, I returned to the words often. In my career as an Army chaplain, I officiated over four hundred military funerals. Each time, I quoted the Twenty-third Psalm. Those veteran's families found assurance in the psalm, as did I.

The Twenty-third Psalm is personal to me. Even though I go through darkness and difficulties that are painful to bear, I am not afraid. God's presence is always greater than my problems. Day by day, God provides whatever I need to endure all the pains and difficulties that I encounter. Simply having His presence beside me is everything I need to get me through the valley.

Is the Twenty-third Psalm personal to you? If you come to Jesus in faith, He will not allow you to walk through your valleys alone. Whether you need to come to the Shepherd for salvation, or you need to come to Him for comfort and renewal, you can come now. He is here. He is waiting.

Chapter 4

Behind Enemy Lines

> *Thou preparest a table before me in the presence of mine enemies: thou anointest my head with oil; my cup runneth over. Surely goodness and mercy shall follow me all the days of my life.*
>
> —Psalm 23:5–6a

On November 27, 1950, Chinese military forces surprised the United States forces at the Chosin Reservoir area in the northeast Korean peninsula. A brutal seventeen-day battle in bitter freezing weather followed. The conflict later became known as the Battle of Chosin Reservoir, and the Americans that fought in the battle were given the nickname "The Chosin Few" because they were greatly outnumbered. There were 120,000 Chinese soldiers compared to the 30,000 United States commanded troops.

One of "The Chosin Few" was a Marine Corps officer named Lewis. In early December 1950, during the most intense combat, Lewis and his men found themselves cut off and surrounded behind enemy lines. The situation looked hopeless. So, Lewis sent a message to his superiors which said, "We've been looking for the enemy for some time now. We've finally found him. We're surrounded. ..."

Can you imagine what it would be like to find yourself outnumbered and surrounded behind enemy lines? If you are a Christian today, you are, in fact, outnumbered and surrounded behind enemy lines. Over my lifetime, I have been amazed at our country's rejection of godly values. We are sheep in the midst of wolves (Matthew 10:16). Satan like a roaring lion is seeking who he can devour (1 Peter 5:8). The enemy takes more ground each day. If you are a Christian in America, you live behind enemy lines in the presence of your enemies.

Sheep live their entire lives behind enemy lines in the presence of their enemies. They are in constant danger from wolves, lions, bears, and snakes. So, sheep need a shepherd to protect them.

David spent much of his life behind enemy lines in the presence of his enemies. Goliath, Saul, the Philistines, and his own son, Absalom, were just a few of the many who tried to kill him. God, like a strong shepherd, had over and over been David's protector behind enemy lines in the presence of his enemies.

In the fifth verse of Psalm 23, we see how God provides for His people behind enemy lines. Now, some theologians see a change between Psalm 23:4 and Psalm 23:5. These scholars believe David changed images. They assert that the first four verses of the Twenty-third Psalm describe God's relationship to David in terms of a shepherd with a sheep. Then, they believe the imagery changed in Psalm 23:5–6 to describe God's relationship to David in terms of a host preparing a banquet for a friend. Some theologians believe that David switched from the pasture to the palace.

However, I see Psalm 23:5–6 continuing with the shepherd sheep relationship. I believe these verses show us the Good Shepherd caring for His flock behind enemy lines.

The Provision Before

The shepherd ensured the provision before the sheep. When David wrote of the Shepherd preparing a *"table"* in the presence of his enemies, he described the shepherd preparing fields for the flock. In the previous chapter, I explained that in the spring, the shepherds in ancient Israel moved their flock to higher ground for the summer. Springtime grazing left the fields bare, so the shepherd sought out new fields. When late summer came, the shepherd moved the sheep to the mountains in search of green pastures. The flat mountain plateaus are called mesas or tables. When David wrote of God preparing a table, he referred to a shepherd leading his sheep to the tablelands, or mountain plateaus. The shepherd would go before the sheep to prepare the "table."

The Hebrew word for "prepare" means *to equip and make ready for battle.* In the Afghanistan and Iraq theaters of the Global War on Terror, many members of the armed forces were killed or injured by improvised explosive devices (IEDs). To clear areas infected with IEDs, the U.S. Army developed a mine-sweeping vehicle called the Buffalo. The Buffalo went before soldiers and cleared the route. That is the word-picture expressed in Psalm 23:5. The shepherd acted as a minesweeper for his flock. He cleared away anything that endangered his sheep.

First, the shepherd went before the flock and looked

for poisonous plants. If the area was overgrown with bad vegetation, the sheep could not graze there. If there was only a small amount of poison plants, the shepherd weeded them out.

Second, the shepherd removed physical hazards like rocks. He filled in holes that might cause the sheep to stumble. He removed obstacles that would injure the flock.

Third, the shepherd searched for signs of predators. The sheep had many natural enemies such as wolves, foxes, bears, eagles, and lions. However, the worst enemy faced by sheep were nose-horned vipers. These venomous snakes made their homes in the tablelands. As the sheep grazed, a viper often struck the sheep's nose. The venom from the bite was fatal.

To combat vipers, shepherds carried a container of oil. They poured the oil around the openings of the snake burrows. This caused the entrances to become slippery, and the snake couldn't easily crawl out. The viper was trapped in his own den.

The shepherd's oil served another purpose described in Psalm 23:5, *"… thou anointest my head with oil."* The shepherd rubbed oil on the head of the sheep. The oil had a smell that repelled vipers. So, because the shepherd poured oil in the entrances of the viper dens and anointed the sheep, the flock were able to graze in the presence of their enemies.

Another enemy the sheep faced were nose flies. The nose fly nested in the sheep's nose where it laid eggs. The eggs hatched a colony of larvae that burrowed deep into the sheep's flesh and caused severe inflammation. The nose flies agitated the sheep, which caused them to stamp their feet erratically and butt their heads against rocks to rid themselves of their misery. The same oil used to repel vipers also repelled nose flies. So, the shepherd applied oil over the sheep's nose and head.

David understood this type of anointing from shepherd to sheep and he, himself, was anointed three times. The prophet Samuel first anointed David when he was a young shepherd (1 Samuel 16:13). Later, the men of Judah anointed David (2 Samuel 2:4). Finally, after the death of Saul, the elders of Israel anointed David as king (2 Samuel 5:3). The shepherd who anointed his sheep with oil was himself anointed to shepherd the flock of Israel.

Sheep Are Defenseless

As I have shown throughout this book, being a shepherd required a commitment to the well-being of the flock. Sheep must have a shepherd to watch over them because they are defenseless. Left alone, sheep will not last very long. Just about every other domesticated animal can be returned to the wild and will stand a fighting chance of survival, but not sheep. If you turn a sheep loose in the wild, you've just given nature a snack.

Sheep do not have claws, fangs, venom, quills, or talons. They have nothing to protect themselves. Sheep are not fast or agile. They cannot outrun a wolf. For defense, dogs will bark, growl, and show their teeth; cats will hiss and arch their back; a rattlesnake will shake his rattle, but the best a sheep can do is *baaa*. I don't think *baaa* will intimidate a predator. Sheep can't fight, they can't run away, and they can't scare away. So, what do sheep do when danger comes? They flock. When a predator comes near, the sheep will gather with others in a pack and run around in circles in complete panic. The only defense they have is the hope that the predator will choose someone else.

Sheep Are Directionless

Sheep are defenseless and they are also directionless. They are prone to wander and get lost. Sheep can even get lost in their own pasture. They have no sense of direction. I am sure you have heard of a lost cat or dog that traveled great distances to find their way home. Cats and dogs know how to get back, but sheep are directionless.

Do you remember the nursery rhyme about Little Bo-Peep? "Little Bo-Peep" is a very famous poem that kids have loved for generations. It opens with these words:

> Little Bo-Peep has lost her sheep,
> And can't tell where to find them;
> Leave them alone, And they'll come home,
> Wagging their tails behind them.

I'm not sure who wrote "Little Bo-Peep," but they didn't know much about sheep. Left alone, sheep will not come home wagging their tails behind them. Sheep are directionless.

Sheep Are Dependent

Sheep are defenseless, directionless, and dependent. They are totally dependent on the shepherd. They can't take care of themselves. They are dependent on the shepherd to go before and provide for them as they move from place to place. When the flock moved to the tablelands in the summer, they were dependent on the shepherd for water.

Remember that sheep will not drink from a running river or stream. They require "still waters" to drink. There were no ponds or sources of "still waters" in the mountain tablelands. So, the shepherd watered the sheep from wells which were often up to one hundred feet deep. The shepherd used a leather bucket that held about three-quarters of a gallon of water. He lowered the bucket into the well and filled a large stone basin with water. The basin was called a cup. The sheep would not stick their head down in the cup. So, the shepherd had to keep it filled to the brim and overflowing. This allowed the sheep to drink with ease. This is the imagery behind *"... my cup runneth over."*

My wife is a coffee connoisseur. We were married in the days before specialty coffee shops. Back then, I used to take her to a little mom-and-pop diner for coffee and pie. It was the kind of place where all the coffee cups had saucers underneath them. The waitress walked over and said, "Whaddaya want, honey?" as she poured our coffee. She always poured the coffee sloppily and it spilled over onto the saucer. My wife used to scold me because I drank the coffee from my saucer because my cup had overflowed.

The Christian life is an overflowing life. God is not stingy. God has a surplus of joy, hope, and peace. The Bible says that God *"is able to do exceeding abundantly above all that we ask or think"* (Ephesians 3:20). In other words, God gives to His children until it overflows.

You may be thinking, "Well, David had an overflowing cup, but you don't know all the problems that I have in my life." It is true, I don't know about all your problems. Still, I would venture to say that you have an overflowing cup.

Several years ago, I read about a man in the midst of

financial collapse who went to his pastor for counseling. "I've lost everything," he said.

The pastor said, "I'm sorry to hear that you've lost your faith."

"No," the man said, "I still have my faith."

The pastor said, "Then I'm sorry to hear that you've lost your character."

The man said, "I never said that. I still have my character."

The pastor said, "Then I'm so sorry to hear that you've lost your salvation."

The man said, "That's not what I said. I didn't lose my salvation."

The pastor said, "So you have your faith, your character, your salvation. It seems to me that you haven't lost anything that really matters."

You may believe that you don't have an overflowing cup, but if you woke up this morning with more health than illness, then you are better off than the million who will not survive this week. If you have food in the refrigerator, clothes on your back, a roof over your head, and a place to sleep, then you are richer than seventy-five percent of this world. If you have money in the bank, in your wallet, and spare change in a dish someplace, then you are among the top eight percent of the world's wealthy. If you are reading this book, then you don't belong to the billion people in the world who cannot read.

Measure your life according to what you have, not what you don't have. Some look at their lives and see only what is not there. All they see is what they lack. Instead, focus on what you have, not what you don't have. Enjoy things for what they are instead of only seeing them for what they aren't. This habit will help you be a little more sheepish as you trust the Shepherd to supply all your needs according to his riches in glory by Christ Jesus (Philippians 4:19). If you are a Christian, you have an overflowing cup.

The Pursuit Behind

Not only did the shepherd ensure the provision before, but he also ensured the pursuit behind. David wrote, *"Surely goodness and mercy shall follow me all the days of my life"* (Psalm 23:6a). When I was a kid, I thought this was three different things—surely, goodness, and mercy. I knew what goodness and mercy were, but I wasn't sure about surely. Someone said that it sounds like a Christian group of attorneys. "I am represented by the law firm of Surely, Goodness, and Mercy …" However, the word "surely" means *certainly* and expresses confidence. In other words, there is no doubt about it. God's goodness and mercy will pursue you all the days of your life.

Goodness speaks of God's benevolence. In church, we often say, "God is good." Someone will then reply, "All the time." That is followed by, "And all the time," with the response of, "God is good." God's goodness is you getting what you do not deserve.

Mercy, on the other hand, is you not getting what you deserve. The Hebrew word for mercy is *hesed,* which means *loving kindness.* It speaks of the covenant loyalty and faithfulness of God. The greatest expression of God's goodness and God's mercy was when His Son, the Lord Jesus Christ came into the world.

I heard about a politician who got elected and went to Washington, DC. When he arrived, he went to the government photography office to have his portrait made. A couple of days later, the proofs arrived at his office. He became very angry with the photographer. He went back to the photography office, stormed in, and said, "This picture does not do me justice." The photographer said, "Sir, with a face like yours, you don't need justice, you need mercy."

I heard about another politician who defined mercy with a court ruling. On a winter night in 1935, Fiorello LaGuardia, the irrepressible mayor of New York, showed up at a night court in the poorest ward of the city. He dismissed the judge for the evening and took over the bench. That night a tattered woman, charged with stealing a loaf of bread, was brought before him. She defended herself and said, "My daughter's husband has deserted her. She is sick, and her children are starving."

The shopkeeper refused to drop the charges. He said, "It's a bad neighborhood, your honor, and she's got to be punished to teach other people a lesson."

LaGuardia sighed. He turned to the old woman and said, "I've got to punish you; the law makes no exceptions. Ten dollars or ten days in jail." However, even while pronouncing sentence, LaGuardia reached into his pocket, took out a ten-dollar bill, and threw it into his hat with these famous words: "Here's the ten-dollar fine, which I now remit, and furthermore, I'm going to fine everyone in this courtroom fifty cents for living in a town where a person has to steal bread so that her grandchildren can eat. Mr. Bailiff, collect the fines and give them to the defendant."

The following day, a New York newspaper reported:

"Forty-seven dollars and fifty cents was turned over to a bewildered old grandmother who stole a loaf of bread to feed her starving grandchildren. Making forced donations were a red-faced storekeeper, seventy petty criminals, and a few New York policemen."

Sometimes we get what we don't deserve. That old grandmother, by the letter of the law, deserved justice, but she got mercy. The truth is we all need mercy. God sent Jesus because I am a sinner, and you are a sinner. The Bible says, *"For all have sinned, and come short of the glory of God."* Because we are sinners, we deserve justice, we deserve Hell. Left to our own, there is nothing we can do to save ourselves. We need a Savior. So, because of His goodness and mercy, God sent Jesus to save us from our sins.

The Bible says God's goodness and mercy *shall follow me.* The imagery here is one of a continuous pursuit. Many ancient shepherds used sheep dogs. While the shepherd led from the front, sheep dogs herded behind and kept the flock in line. David illustrated God's relationship to the believer with that word-picture. Your Shepherd is out ahead preparing the table while His goodness and mercy are following behind, always on your trail all the days of your life.

I served as a U.S. Army chaplain for many years. Most people do not know that military chaplains are non-combatants. I was not allowed to carry a weapon. Since I could not defend myself, a chaplain assistant had the assignment to protect me—sort of like how a Secret Service agent protects the President of the United States. In 2010, I deployed to Iraq in support of Operation Iraqi Freedom. There must have been a surplus of chaplain assistants that year, because instead of the usual one, three chaplain assistants were assigned – Private Aaron Chrisman, Sergeant Joseph White, and Sergeant Ricky Warren. Since it was their job to keep me safe, those three men followed me everywhere. Some of the other soldiers called them Private Surely, Sergeant Goodness, and Sergeant Mercy because they followed me all the days of my life.

Those three men always followed on my heels, but that is nothing compared to the goodness and mercy of God. The Bible says goodness and mercy will follow you *"all the days"* of your life. There will not be a single day in which His faithful favor will not be close behind you. These two parts of God's love will nip at your heels all day, every day, for the rest of your life. There will never be a moment in which the goodness and mercy of the Lord will not be immediately nearby. You can never escape the loyal love of the Good Shepherd, even when you are surrounded and outnumbered behind enemy lines.

I started this chapter with the story of a Marine named Lewis who found himself cut-off, surrounded, and out-numbered behind enemy lines during the Korean War at the Battle of Chosin Reservoir. Lewis sent a message to his superiors which said, "We've been looking for the enemy for some time now. We've finally found him. We're sur-rounded ..." There was a pause, and the confident Marine finished his sentence, "that simplifies things."

Lewis was actually excited to find himself in what seemed like a hopeless situation. You see, Lewis had been in similar situations before. He started his military career fighting guerillas in Haiti and Nicaragua as part of the Banana Wars. He later served with distinction in World War

II. He had been in the presence of his enemies many times before. So, at the Battle of the Chosin Reservoir, Lewis said, "They are in front of us, and we are flanked on both sides by an enemy that outnumbers us 29-to-1. They can't get away from us now!"

Lewis, who said those famous words, was Lewis Burwell "Chesty" Puller. He went on to command the 1st Marine Division to victory at Chosin. The Marines inflicted the highest casualty ratio on an enemy in history and destroyed seven enemy divisions in the process. For his actions, "Chesty" Puller was awarded the Distinguished Service Cross from the U.S. Army, and his fifth Navy Cross for heroism. He retired from the Marine Corps in 1955 at the rank of Major General as the most decorated Marine in American history.

Knowing the enemy surrounds you is helpful. Attacking the enemy with everything you have is even *more* helpful. How are you waging war right now? Have faith in the trenches and stay focused on our Commander. He will fight for you until the last battle is won.

Chapter 5

The Best Is Yet to Come

*...and I will dwell in the house of the L*ORD *for ever.*
—Psalm 23:6b

The final benefit of having the Lord as your Shepherd is a heavenly home. I once heard a preacher describe these last words in the Twenty-third Psalm. He said, "David knew that he was not only loved by the Father's heart, and held by the Father's hand, but that someday, he would be welcomed into the Father's house." David looked forward to living happily ever after.

As a child, my grandmother (I called her Mimmie) used to read fairy tales to me. I loved spending the night at Mimmie's house and listening before bed as she read stories. The story I most fondly remember is *The Three Little Pigs*. She used to make the noise of the big bad wolf as he huffed and puffed to blow the houses down. I enjoyed hearing about the third pig, who built his house out of bricks and outsmarted the wolf. What I think I remember most about ALL of the fairy tales Mimmie read to me is that in some way, shape, or form, they all ended happily ever after

... well, unless you were the wolf or some other villain. Still, to this day, I love the idea of living happily ever after.

All the great fairy tales ended with happily ever after. Cinderella escaped the harsh life with her cruel stepmother and stepsisters and married a prince. Jack escaped poverty with the riches he took from the giant's castle and managed to chop down the beanstalk before the giant could catch him. Rapunzel and her prince were reunited, and her magical tears even cured his blindness. Pinocchio was transformed into a real boy by a fairy. And they all lived happily ever after.

However, the Bible is not a fairy tale. God's Word is truth, and the truth is, if you are a believer, you will live happily ever after in a place called Heaven. David knew this truth and used the shepherd/sheep image to look forward to a day when he journeyed to the house of the Lord.

When we come to the end of the Twenty-third Psalm, we have come full circle. The psalm opened in the late winter or early spring with the shepherd keeping his flock. As spring merged into summer, the shepherd moved the flock north to higher ground. As they made their way from the lower lands to the tablelands, they traveled through some dark valleys. As we come to the last verse, the summer is nearly over, and the fall and winter are coming. So, the shepherd took his sheep back home.

The Certainty of Heaven

I have two simple points to guide us as we look at our heavenly home. First, there is the certainty of Heaven. David said, *"... and I will dwell in the house of the LORD for ever."* He didn't say, "might" or "hope to." He said, "I will." David had no doubt that he would be in the house of the Lord when he died. Christians have the same certainty. One way or another, believers will be in Heaven for all eternity.

The Reality of the Rapture

I love the story of the elderly man who volunteered to help with Vacation Bible School (VBS) at his church. He was assigned to help with the preschool class. The man wanted to teach the gospel to the children in a memorable way. So, he asked those four- and five-year-olds, "Can any of you tell me what I've got to do to get to Heaven?" Nobody answered. The kids just silently looked at him.

He said, "What if I sold my house and my car and gave all the money to the church? Would that get me to Heaven?"

All the children perked up and yelled, "No!"

The man said, "What if I was a good person and obeyed all the laws of the land like a good citizen? Would that get me to Heaven?"

All the little boys and girls screamed, "No!"

He asked, "What if I loved my wife with all my heart? Would that get me to Heaven?"

All the kids yelled out, "No!"

Finally, the man said, "Well, will one of you tell me what I've got to do to get to Heaven?"

A little five-year-old boy jumped up and said, "You've got to die, old man. You've got to die!"

However, the little boy was wrong. Not everybody will die to get to Heaven. Some will go to Heaven without going through the graveyard. Some will go to Heaven without having a funeral. Some will fly instead of die. Some people will be caught up to meet the Lord Jesus Christ in the Rapture.

The Apostle Paul described the Rapture in his first letter to the Church in Thessalonica:

For the Lord himself shall descend from heaven with a shout, with the voice of the archangel, and with the trump of God: and the dead in Christ shall rise first: Then we which are alive and remain shall be caught up together with them in the clouds, to meet the Lord in the air: and so shall we ever be with the Lord. Wherefore comfort one another with these words.
—1 Thessalonians 4:16–18

Someday, Jesus will descend from Heaven with a shout. Did you know every time Jesus shouted in the Bible, dead people got up? He shouted at the tomb of Lazarus, and Lazarus got up. He shouted on the cross, and dead people got up. He will shout one more time, and the dead in Christ will rise.

The Bible says Jesus will come, *"with the voice of the archangel."* The only angel in the Bible that is given the title of archangel is Michael. Michael is going to lift his voice. Some believe he is assembling the other angels to war as the Tribulation breaks loose on this planet. That could be true, but I believe it is also a shout of victory. It is a shout of praise to the Lord Jesus Christ.

The Bible says He will come, *"with the trump of God."* This trumpet is the ram's horn—the shofar. Trumpets were used to call armies to assemble and march. Also, trumpets were used to announce the appearance of royalty. Here He is! Here is royalty. Jesus is the King of Kings. He is the Lord of Lords. He is the King of Glory. He is royalty and He will be announced by a trumpet.

My favorite word in 1 Thessalonians 4:17 is "we." Oh, Lord God, I pray that I am still a "we" at that time. I so want to see the Rapture. Won't it be exciting when we will all be changed? I don't know about you, but I look forward to the day when we drop these old worn-out bodies, and we put on a brand-new body.

We will be changed in the twinkling of an eye. That is faster than the speed of light. Faster than the speed of light, there will be no more aches and pains. Faster than the speed of light, we will live in a world with no more abortion. Faster than the speed of light, we will live in a world with no more cemeteries. Faster than the speed of light, we will live in a world with no more death. Faster than the speed of light, we will meet Jesus in the air.

No, not everybody will die to get to Heaven. Some believers will be caught up in the Rapture.

The Reality of the Resurrection

Until the Rapture, we still live in a world that is cursed with death. If the Lord does not return within our lifetime, you and I will die. However, if you are a believer, when you die, you will be absent from the body and present with the Lord (2 Corinthians 5:6) where you will await the resurrection. When the Lord returns for His church, the dead in Christ shall rise (1 Thessalonians 4:16). At the resurrection of believers, the physical body is resurrected, glorified, and then reunited with the soul/spirit.

We get a glimpse of what our resurrected bodies will be like when we examine Jesus' post-resurrection appearances.

He could be physically touched, but He was able to travel effortlessly and appear and disappear at will. He could go through walls and doors, but could also eat, drink, sit, and talk. The Bible says our "vile" bodies will be just like His "glorious body" (Philippians 3:21) and we will live forever with the Lord.

Sadly, for some, the resurrection will not be a pleasant experience. The Bible says all people will be resurrected, some to "everlasting life," others to shame and "everlasting contempt." or death (Daniel 12:2). Everyone will be removed—period, but there will be two different destinies. The difference is faith in Christ. Believers will ultimately be granted entrance into the New Heavens and New Earth (Revelation 21:1). Unbelievers will be sent to the lake of fire (Revelation 20:11-15).

David confidently wrote, "... and I will dwell in the house of the LORD for ever." He didn't say, "... then." He said, "... and." It was not a matter of, "Surely goodness and mercy shall follow you all the days of your life. Then when you die you will dwell in the house of the Lord." That is not how David saw it. He saw it as seamless. Take one step. Take another step. The next step after is death. He said "and"— not "then"—"... and I will dwell in the house of the LORD for ever."

The Company of Heaven

So, you can be sure of the certainty of Heaven, and you can look forward to the company of Heaven. David called Heaven *"the house of the Lord."* It's not just anybody's house. It's the Lord's house. Jesus said, *"In my Father's house are many mansions: if it were not so, I would have told you. I go to pre-pare a place for you"* (John 14:2). The Shepherd of your soul will take care of you every day of your life. He will meet your every need. Then, at the end of this life, Jesus will take you to the Father's house where you will live forever.

Your Loved Ones Are in the House
Jesus said that He went to prepare a place for His followers (John 14:2). Other believers will be in Heaven too. Mark Twain once said, "I'll take Heaven for the climate, but Hell for the company." I don't know about you, but I'll take Heaven for both. Heaven is a place where the people of God will be together.

Jesus gave us a glimpse into Heaven and Hell in his teaching on the rich man and Lazarus (Luke 16:19–31). Lazarus died and the angels came and carried him to Abraham's bosom. The rich man also died and was buried. The tormented rich man in Hell saw Lazarus in Heaven. He cried out to Abraham for mercy. The rich man begged Abraham to send Lazarus to his five brothers to warn them so they would not *"come into this place of torment."* The rich man was concerned about his brothers being tormented. Hell is a place of eternal torment.

Well, Mr. Mark Twain, so much for the company of Hell.

Heaven, on the other hand, is a place of eternal happiness. One of the greatest joys will be our reunion with our loved ones who have gone there before us. When King David's infant son died, David grieved his loss, but he also knew he would see him again. David declared, *"I shall go to him, but he shall not return to me."* (2 Samuel 12:23).

When Jesus was transfigured (or changed) before the eyes of some of His disciples and they glimpsed His heavenly glory, Moses and Elijah appeared with Him. This is proof that we retain our individuality in Heaven (see Luke 9:28–36). Later, while sharing the Passover meal with His disciples, Jesus said, *"I will not drink of the fruit of the vine, until the kingdom of God shall come."* (Luke 22:18). Christ promised that He and His disciples would drink the fruit of the vine together again in Heaven. Individual believers will recognize and know each other when we are reunited in Heaven.

Dr. R. G. Lee was the much-loved pastor of Bellevue Baptist Church in Memphis from 1927 to 1960. One day, when R. G. was a little boy, he asked his mother, Elizabeth, what was the happiest day of her life. She thought back to the time of the Civil War when she was a little girl. Elizabeth's father had fought for the South. While he was away, her mother had to do all the work in the fields. One day a letter arrived that said her father had been killed in battle. Elizabeth's mother didn't cry much that day, but the children heard her sobbing at night in their small house.

About four months later, Elizabeth's family sat one day on the front porch shelling beans. A man walked down the road and Elizabeth's mother watched him for a while. She said, "Elizabeth, that man coming yonder walks like your father."

The man kept coming down the road, but the children thought, "It can't be him." Then as he came to the break in the fence, he turned in. Her mother jumped up and cried, "Children, it is your father!"

Elizabeth's mother ran all the way across the field, kissed her husband, cried, and held him for the longest time. Many years later, Elizabeth told her son, "It was the happiest hour I ever knew."

That is just a taste, just a hint of the joy-filled future in store for all who have received Jesus as Savior and Lord. It will be a glorious day when we are reunited with our loved ones in Heaven.

Your Lord Is In the House

In the Old Testament, the house of the Lord is mentioned many times. Most often, the house of the Lord referred to the tabernacle or the temple. The house of the Lord was the place where God dwelled among His people. David knew he would live in the presence of the Lord forever.

When I think of my home, I don't think of the house, my chair, and my television. Those are just things. When I think of my home, I think of my wife and children. Where they are is my home. Where they are is where I want to be. They make home … home. What makes Heaven Heaven? Jesus.

The best thing about Heaven is the presence of our Lord and Savior (1 John 3:2). We will be face-to-face with the Lamb of God who loved us and sacrificed Himself so that we can enjoy His presence in Heaven for eternity.

Psalm 23 begins with the words, "The LORD" and it ends with "the LORD for ever." It starts with the Lord, and it ends with the Lord forever. The focus throughout the psalm is on the Shepherd. Heaven is all about Jesus.

Not too long ago, a young woman was diagnosed with a terminal illness. Doctors gave her three months to live. As she worked to get her things "in order," she contacted her pastor and had him come to her house to discuss her funeral. She told him which songs she wanted sang at the service, what scriptures she would like read, and what outfit she wanted to be buried in.

Everything was in order. As the pastor prepared to leave the young woman suddenly remembered something very important to her. She said, "There's one more thing."

The pastor said, "What's that?"

She said, "I want to be buried with a fork in my right hand."

The pastor looked at her and he didn't know what to say. So, she spoke up and said, "That surprises you, doesn't it?"

He said, "Well, to be honest, I'm puzzled by the request. I have never had anyone ask to be buried with a fork in their right hand."

The young woman smiled and explained, "My grandmother used to tell me about all her years of going to church socials and potluck dinners. She said that she always remembered when the dishes of the main course were being cleared, someone would lean over and say, 'Keep your fork!' It was my grandma's favorite part because she knew something better was coming. The best part of the meal was yet to come, like velvety chocolate cake or deep-dish apple pie. The best was yet to come."

The young woman smiled at her pastor and said, "So, I just want people to see me there in that casket with a fork in my hand and I want them to wonder 'What's with the fork?' Then I want you to tell them: 'Keep your fork the best is yet to come.'"

For the Christian, the best is yet to come. If the Lord should come and take us in the clouds, or if death takes us, we will go where all are forever young. We will go where there are no wrinkles. We will go where there are no deformed bodies. We will go where there are no crippled limbs. In the twinkling of an eye—in less than a second—we will be in a place where there are no wheelchairs, no walkers, no hospitals, no broken relationships, no heartaches, no pain, and no death. We are going to a place where we will never have to walk through a valley of darkness, because the Lord Jesus Christ will be the light.

Psalm 23 ends with a reminder that the best is yet to come. If the Lord is your Shepherd, you will never lack for anything you really need … forever.

Shepherds and the Lamb

> *And there were in the same country shepherds abiding in the field, keeping watch over their flock by night. And, lo, the angel of the Lord came upon them, and the glory of the Lord shone round about them: and they were sore afraid. And the angel said unto them, Fear not: for, behold, I bring you good tidings of great joy, which shall be to all people. For unto you is born this day in the city of David a Saviour, which is Christ the Lord.*
>
> —Luke 2:8–11

S hepherds have a special place in the Bible. As we have seen, David was a shepherd. Abraham, Isaac, and Jacob kept sheep. Joseph's family took their sheep to Egypt, even though the Egyptians despised shepherds. Moses was a shepherd. The prophet Amos tended sheep. God holds shepherds in high regard.

God's high regard for shepherds is found in the writing of the prophet Isaiah. He compared the Lord to a shepherd when he wrote, *"He shall feed his flock like a shepherd: he shall gather the lambs with his arm, and carry them in his bosom, and shall gently lead those that are with young"* (Isaiah 40:11). You also see God's high regard for shepherd in the teachings of Jesus, who said, *"I am the good shepherd: the good shepherd giveth his life for the sheep"* (John 10:11).

Every Christmas we remember the special place God has for shepherds. As Luke tells us, even though Bethlehem was so full of people that there was no room for Mary and Joseph to stay, who did the angels tell a Savior had been born that very day, and that they would find him wrapped in cloths and lying in a manger? It was shepherds. Why shepherds? Yes, they were in fields nearby, but there were many other people who would have been even closer, and yes, they were awake, keeping watch over their flocks that night. Still, God could have awakened anyone He wanted; a multitude of angels tends to have that effect on you. Yet God chose to reveal the birth of his Son to the shepherds because it is the heart of God to be a shepherd.

The Mishnah was the first written record of Jewish oral traditions. It is also known as the "Oral Torah." *The Mishnah* stipulated that all the flocks be kept in the wilderness, except the flocks used for the temple services which were kept at Bethlehem. The Bethlehem shepherds were responsible to care for the sacrificial lambs, many of which would become Passover lambs, when the ultimate Passover Lamb was born.

Now this is not a Christmas book, but if you will permit me, I want to take you back to the first Christmas. Let's look at the significance of the shepherds to understand the reasons God chose them to be His messengers of the manger.

Extraordinary Messengers

And it came to pass, as the angels were gone away from them into heaven, the shepherds said one to another, Let us now go even unto Bethlehem, and see this thing which is come to pass, which the Lord hath made known unto us.

—Luke 2:15

What is the best news you have ever received? How did you react when you heard it? Did it produce excitement, or did it bring peace? Was there a feeling of exhilaration, or did a calm feeling settle over you? Perhaps you have experienced some or all these emotions and maybe even more.

There have been times when I received wonderful news in my life. It was wonderful news when my wife, Amanda, said "yes" to marrying me. It was wonderful news when Amanda said, "We are going to have a baby"—all three times. It was wonderful news, when I was serving in the U.S. Army in a war far from home and the commander came and said, "We are going home." Each of those incidents were good news.

However, the best news you or I ever received pales in comparison to the news the angel gave to the shepherds some two thousand or so years ago. The angel said, *"Fear not: for, behold, I bring you good tidings of great joy, which shall be to all people. For unto you is born this day in the city of David a Saviour, which is Christ the Lord."* The shepherds received the best news anyone in the world had ever received—God came to earth in the Person of Jesus Christ.

On July 29, 1969, astronaut Neil Armstrong climbed down a ladder and put his feet on the surface of the moon.

In an address, President Richard Nixon said, "The greatest event in human history occurred when man first put his foot on the moon." Astronaut Hale Irwin responded to Nixon's comments, "The most significant achievement of our age is not that man stood on the moon, but rather that God in Christ stood on the earth." That is the greatest news in all of history.

Shepherds were the first to receive the greatest news in all of history. These social outcasts were unlikely candidates to be presented with the birth announcement of Christ because shepherds were despised in the time of Jesus. However, that was not always the case. Shepherds were not always despised. As we have already discussed, David was a shepherd. Being a shepherd was a wonderful profession in the Old Testament, but not in the day of Christ. The Pharisees, the Sadducees, and the religious rulers despised shepherds because they couldn't keep all their religious rules. In order to be religiously pure, you had to do all this ceremonial washing, and keep all these rules. Shepherds had to work outside in the fields. They couldn't keep all the rules.

Religion, man-made tradition, ruins people. Religion is man's attempt to be right with God with his own good works. Religion is man trying to earn his way into heaven. Religion is spelled D-O. Christianity is spelled D-O-N-E. People can sit in church their entire life and die and go to Hell because they are blinded by the human traditions of men. They are blinded by religion.

The shepherds outside of Bethlehem tended the very flocks that were used in the sacrifices of Jerusalem. These shepherds took care of the lambs that were offered in the name of religion, but they were despised and not allowed in the temple. God sent the message to these shepherds because they had not been ruined by religion.

And this shall be a sign unto you; Ye shall find the babe wrapped in swaddling clothes, lying in a manger.

—Luke 2:12

A baby "wrapped in swaddling clothes, lying in a manger" sounds strange to us today. However, it would not have sounded strange to the shepherds. In Genesis 35:21 we read, "*And Israel journeyed, and spread his tent beyond the tower of Eder.*" This passage has to do with the burial of Jacob's wife, Rachel. She was buried in Bethlehem (Genesis 35:19). After his wife's burial, Jacob camped near Bethlehem in a place beyond what the Hebrew calls *Migdal Eder* or the Tower of Eder.

The Tower of Eder was originally built as a military outpost outside of Bethlehem for the protection of Jerusalem located six miles away. Later, King Solomon moved the military garrison and changed the name of the Tower of Eder to the Tower of the Flock because it was used by the shepherds.

The Tower of the Flock was a three-story structure. The shepherds watched over their flocks from the top story, the second story was used for storage, and the bottom story was used as a birthing chamber. Each time an ewe was ready to give birth, the shepherds took her out of the valley and up the hill to the Tower of the Flock. When the ewe delivered, the baby lamb was cleaned up and wrapped with swaddling clothes to restrict it from moving.

After the newborn lamb was swaddled, it was carried into the inner chamber of the Tower of the Flock. There, the lamb was laid inside a stone manger. The little lamb remained in the manger until he was inspected for spot or blemish by the chief shepherd. If the lamb was acceptable, it was taken back to its mother and back to the flock. As the lamb grew, if it developed no spot or blemish, it would be used as a sacrifice in the temple.

The shepherds knew exactly what to look for when they heard the angel say that they would find a baby *"wrapped in swaddling clothes, lying in a manger."* The Lord Jesus Christ was born in the shadow of the Tower of the Flock. He was born in the same place as the sacrificial lambs. He was wrapped in the same clothes as the sacrificial lambs. He was laid in the same kind of manger as the sacrificial lambs. No wonder John the Baptist said about Him, *"Behold the Lamb of God, which taketh away the sin of the world"* (John 1:29b).

Seven hundred years before Jesus was born, the prophet Micah, under the inspiration of the Holy Spirit wrote, *"But thou, Bethlehem Ephratah, though thou be little among the thousands of Judah, yet out of thee shall he come forth unto me that is to be ruler in Israel; whose goings forth have been from of old, from everlasting"* (Micah 5:2). This amazing prophecy predicts the exact birthplace of the Messiah. However, Micah dug down deeper when he wrote, *"And thou, O tower of the flock, the strong hold of the daughter of Zion, unto thee shall it come, even the first dominion; the kingdom shall come to the daughter of Jerusalem"* (Micah 4:8). Seven hundred years before His birth, Micah said Jesus would be born in Bethlehem, specifically mentioning the Tower of the Flock.

A four-year-old girl often forgot to close the door when

coming in from outside. Finally, her father scolded her, "Shut that door! Were you born in a barn?" She looked at her father and replied softly, "No, but Jesus was."

Jesus was born in a barn. Mary had a little Lamb in a barn. She wrapped the Lamb in swaddling clothes and placed Him in a stone manger. When the Bethlehem shepherds came to inspect the Lamb, they found Him lying in the manger.

And they came with haste, and found Mary, and Joseph, and the babe lying in a manger.

—Luke 2:16

The shepherds came with haste. They were in a hurry. They came with haste and "found"—that means they were searching.

Have you searched your entire life? You thought your search had ended in a relationship, but that was a disaster. You thought your search had ended in a job, but that didn't work out. You thought your search had ended in a pill, something you sniffed up your nose, or in a bottle, but all that only left you depressed and miserable. You thought your search had ended in money, but that came up empty.

Today, if you will humble yourself, your search can be over. The only One Who can satisfy the longing and emptiness of your soul is Jesus Christ.

Excited Messengers

And when they had seen it, they made known abroad the saying which was told them concerning this child.

—Luke 2:17

The shepherds shared the message. They shared the good news that Jesus Christ was born. They didn't worry about how it was received. They didn't worry if people believed it. They didn't worry if people accepted it. Their job was to just deliver the message. That's what God has called us to do. It's not complicated. All you must do is tell people about your experience with Jesus Christ and leave the results in the hands of God.

The Bible says the shepherds made the good news known abroad. They were excited about the message. It's a message that still excites me. I was going to Hell, but now I am saved. There was a load of sin crushing me, and now it is lifted off me. My heart was empty and now it's full of Jesus. When I die, I'm not going to die. One day, I will stand in the eternal presence of Jesus Christ. God loved me so much that He sent His Son to save my soul. That's something to get excited about.

Are you excited?

And all they that heard it wondered at those things which were told them by the shepherds.
—Luke 2:18

Two thousand years ago, shepherds were not permitted to testify in court, but God used humble shepherds to be the first human witnesses that prophecy was fulfilled and the Messiah was born. God used shepherds because they would understand that the Savior, lying in the quiet manger, was to be the Lamb of God. As the Lamb, He would die for the sins of the world. He died for these very shepherds. God used shepherds, who cared for the young lambs, who sat through cold dark nights in the fields to guard and protect their flocks, because they understood the shepherd's heart of the Father and what it meant for Him to give His one Lamb for all.

The shepherds became the first evangelists when they shared the good news. The people who heard them "wondered" at the things the shepherds said. They were amazed the Messiah was born in a stable and not in a palace, and angels brought news of His birth to poor shepherds and not to the chief priests.

But Mary kept all these things, and pondered them in her heart.
—Luke 2:19

Several years ago, a young mother named Susan was released from the hospital after extensive rounds of therapy failed to turn back the progress of a deadly disease. Confined to her bed at home, she received regular visits from her physician, but she couldn't work up the courage to explain her illness to her six-year-old daughter.

One morning, the little girl overheard the doctor speaking with her mother and father. "I'll be frank with you, Susan," the physician said, "you don't have much time. I don't think you'll survive the autumn." A short while later, Susan glanced out the bedroom window and saw something that nearly broke her heart. She watched as her daughter bent to pick up the leaves that had begun to fall in the September breeze; and then, as if to foil the force of gravity itself, the little girl worked to scotch-tape each leaf back on a branch. She tried to keep autumn from coming.

I wonder sometimes if Mary wished she could do

something like that. Mary "kept" and "pondered" in her heart that her Baby was the Messiah. As she raised Jesus, watched Him grow, and understood more and more of His mission here on earth, she must have wanted to turn back the clock. She knew He was born to be the Lamb of God, and He would die as a sacrifice for sin.

Mary "kept" all these things and "pondered" them in her heart. The word for "kept" means *preserved*. She preserved them in her heart. The word for "pondered" literally means *to throw together*. Mary absorbed all that happened around her and threw all the images and sounds and smells together to create a treasure in her heart.

In 1984, Jerry Falwell called singer, songwriter, Mark Lowry and asked him to write the script for Liberty University's annual Christmas program. As he worked on the program, Lowry had a conversation with his mother. She said, "If anyone on earth knew for sure that Jesus was virgin born—Mary knew!" His mother's statement stuck with Lowry. He wrote out a list of questions he would like to ask Mary if he could sit down with her. The questions Lowry wrote eventually became the wonderful Christmas song, *Mary, Did You Know?*

One of the lyrics of *Mary, Did You Know?* asks the question, "Mary, did you know that your baby boy is Heaven's perfect lamb?"

Mary knew.

She knew that His hands so tiny on his birth night, would one day be pierced in two by nails.

She knew that Jesus was born to be the sacrificial Lamb to take away the sins of the world, and she "kept" and "pondered" it in her heart.

Everyday Messengers

*And the shepherds returned, glorifying and praising God for all
the things that they had heard and seen, as it was told unto them.*
—Luke 2:20

The shepherds "returned." They returned to their jobs—to
being shepherds. It was an old job, but they were new men.
Now they had Jesus in their hearts and praise on their lips.

God wants you to go back to your job tomorrow. God
wants you to go to your classroom. God wants you to go
back to your life.

You might think, "I've got an ordinary life." Quit thinking like that! You are a messenger of God. Our responsibil-
ity is to make Christ known wherever we might be. Go out
and be a new man, a new woman, full of the Lord. One
of the marks of a genuine Christian is a joyful confession
of faith. An everyday place becomes an extraordinary place
when there is a believer there full of Christ.

Don Bakely once pastored a church in urban Camden,
New Jersey. At the time he pastored the church, Camden
was named the nation's most dangerous city. He was especially concerned about a man named "Big Mart." One day,
Pastor Bakely was sitting in his church office when he
heard a commotion outside. He heard profanity, shout-
ing, a loud argument. The argument was between Ella, the
church secretary, and Big Mart. Big Mart was calling Ella
a vile and obscene name. Before the pastor could respond,
Ella came storming into his office.

She said, "Did you hear what that young man called me out there?" When he replied that he had, Ella asked, "Well, what are you going to do about it?" Pastor Bakely said, "That's a good question, Ella—a really good question. But the real question is what are you going to do about it?"

Ella had not expected that kind of an answer, but she regrouped and with some exasperation she said, "I guess I want you to go out there and throw him out." Pastor Bakely quickly replied, "Ella, I have been working for six weeks to get him in here. You want me to throw him out on the first day?"

The pastor continued, "Ella, let me tell you a story: it's a true story: then I want you to go home and think about it.

"When Big Mart was a little boy, his dad came home one night in a rage and began to beat up his mother. In a violent frenzy, he shoved the children into the room, closed the door, and forced them to watch while he killed their mother. He then took a paring knife and cut her head off her dead body. He decapitated their mother in front of those children. When Big Mart could not stand it anymore, he broke for the door and got out, but when he reached the top of the stairs, his father threw his mother's head and hit him in the back. The force of the blow knocked Big Mart down the stairs. When he woke up, he was lying on his mother's head. That's Big Mart. That's the guy you met out there. That's the guy who called you that name."

Ella didn't say a word. She turned and walked out the door, but she was back in twenty minutes. She walked over to the pastor's desk and looked at him. The pastor said, "Well?" And she said, "I guess I'm going to have to learn how to get cussed out."

Are there any "Big Mart's" in your life? How do you relate to them? Do you have a burden deep in your soul for them?

The good news of great joy is not just for church people. It's not just for "good people." The good news of great joy is for all people ... Rich people. Poor people. People who struggle to make ends meet. People with serious health issues. People who are healthy and strong. Single people. Divorced people. Married. Widowed. Educated. Uneducated. Conservative. Liberal. Young. Old. Black. White. Beautiful. Ugly. All people.

The good news of great joy is for all people.

Accept It

How do you respond to the good news? The shepherds are a great example of how to respond. First, you should accept it. When the angels finished delivering their good news, the shepherds believed. They didn't argue among themselves, question what the angel said, or try to understand what the angel said. They just believed.

One important, basic response we should have to this good news of great joy is to accept it. Simply accept it.

Understand that to accept something doesn't mean we have to understand it. I don't understand how God could become a man, but I accept it. I don't understand how Jesus could be born of a virgin, but I accept it. I responded to this good news by simply believing it. That is called faith. It was the same faith that enabled me to trust Jesus for my salvation.

Adhere to It

Our second response to the good news is adhere to it. The

angel told the shepherds the Christ Child would be found in the City of David. The message was so important to the shepherds that they hurried and adhered without haste.

Announce It

The third response to this good news is to announce it. When the shepherds saw the Christ Child, they began to share with others this good news of great joy. They announced exactly what they had heard, and exactly what they had seen. Once they had seen the Christ Child, they could hardly speak of anything else.

If you are a believer, you are commanded to be a faithful witness. What should you say? Just announce what you have seen and heard in your life as a Christian. Tell what Christ has done for you in the past. Tell what Christ is doing right now in the present. Tell what Christ will do for you in the future. Respond to the good news of great joy by announcing the news to others.

Well, there you have it. Maybe now you understand why the greatest announcement ever made to the world was given to humble shepherds. It was as if God reminded us that night what kind of care He wants for His people and who He wanted to provide it. Not the rich temple leaders who were taking advantage of His flock. Not the proud Pharisees who despised the outcast "sheep." But caring shepherds with humble hearts that daily provide the sheep with good grass and clean water while protecting, leading, and guiding them.

I think another reason shepherds were the first to hear the good news that night is because many years later, Jesus would call Himself the Good Shepherd (John 10:11). It all fits. He is the Good Shepherd, the Great Shepherd, the Chief Shepherd. The Lord Jesus Christ is my Shepherd. That is why God holds shepherds in such high regard.

Not only is Jesus the Shepherd, in some way that only God could work out, He is also the Lamb. When John the Baptist saw Jesus coming, he said, *"Behold, the Lamb of God … "* (John 1:29). The people of Christ's day understood the sacrificial lamb. They would have immediately thought of any one of several important sacrifices. With the time of the Passover feast being very near, their first thought might be the sacrifice of the Passover lamb.

The Passover feast was one of the main Jewish holidays and a celebration in remembrance of God's deliverance of the Israelites from bondage in Egypt. In fact, the slaying of the Passover lamb and the applying of the blood to door-posts of the houses (Exodus 12:11–13) is a beautiful picture of Christ's atoning work on the cross. Those for whom He died are covered by His blood, protecting us from the angel of (spiritual) death.

Not only did the people of Christ's day understand the Passover, they also understood the daily sacrifice at the temple in Jerusalem. Every morning and evening, a lamb was sacrificed in the temple for the sins of the people (Exodus 29:38–42). These daily sacrifices, like all others, were simply to point people towards the perfect sacrifice of Christ on the cross. In fact, the time of Jesus' death on the cross corresponds to the time the evening sacrifice was being made in the temple.

The Jews at that time would have also been familiar with the Old Testament prophets, specifically Jeremiah and Isaiah who prophesied that the coming Messiah would suffer and be sacrificed. Jeremiah foretold the coming of One who would be like a lamb *"brought to the slaughter"* (Jeremiah 11:19). Isaiah described Christ's silence before His accusers and used the imagery of a lamb being slaughtered. He wrote, *"He was oppressed, and he was afflicted, yet he opened not his mouth: he is brought as a lamb to the slaughter, and as a sheep before her shearers is dumb, so he openeth not his mouth"* (Isaiah 53:7).

Did you know sheep will not fight the person who is taking them into the slaughterhouse? Sheep will not defend themselves. In fact, a sheep will lean over and lick the hand of the man in the slaughterhouse that slits their throat. As the blood begins to flow away from the dying sheep, it will lovingly, like a pet dog, lick the hand of the man who is killing it. The prophets Jeremiah and Isaiah used that image to describe Jesus Christ—an image the people of the time understood.

While the idea of a sacrificial system might seem strange to us today, the concept of payment or restitution is still one we can easily understand. We know that the *"wages of sin is death"* (Romans 6:23) and that our sin separates us from God. We also know the Bible teaches we are all sinners and none of us is righteous before God (Romans 3:23). Because of our sin, we are separated from God, and we stand guilty before Him. Therefore, the only hope we can have is if He provides a way for us to be reconciled to Himself, and that is what He did in sending His Son Jesus Christ to be our sacrificial Lamb. Jesus came to die on the cross. Christ died to make atonement for sin and to pay the penalty of the sins of all who believe in Him.

It is through His death on the cross as God's perfect

sacrifice for sin and His resurrection three days later that you can now have eternal life, if you believe in Him. The fact that God Himself provided the offering that atones for our sin is part of the glorious good news of the gospel that is so clearly declared in 1 Peter 1:18–21:

> *Forasmuch as ye know that ye were not redeemed with corruptible things, as silver and gold, from your vain conversation received by tradition from your fathers; But with the precious blood of Christ, as of **a lamb without blemish and without spot**: Who verily was foreordained before the foundation of the world, but was manifest in these last times for you, Who by him do believe in God, that raised him up from the dead, and gave him glory; that your faith and hope might be in God.*

The Lamb of God wants to be your Shepherd. Would you receive Christ today?

How to Receive Jesus Christ

1. Admit your need (I am a sinner).
2. Be willing to turn from your sins (repent).
3. Believe that Jesus died for you and rose from the grave.
4. Through prayer, invite Jesus Christ to come in and control your life through the Holy Spirit (receive Him as Lord and Savior).

What to Pray

Dear Lord Jesus,

I know that I am a sinner and I need Your forgiveness. I believe that You died for my sins. I want to turn from my sins. I now invite You to come into my heart and life. I want to trust and follow You as Lord and Savior.

In Jesus' Name. Amen.

Bibliography

Church, J.R. *Hidden Prophecies in the Psalms.* Oklahoma City: Prophecy Publications, 1986.

Evans, Tony. *God Is More Than Enough.* Colorado Springs: Multnomah Publishing, 2004.

Keller, Phillip. *A Shepherd Looks at Psalm 23.* Minneapolis: World Wide Publications, 1970.

Meyer, F.B. *The Shepherd Psalm.* Fort Washington, PA: Christian Literature Crusade, 1972.

McGee, J. Vernon. *Through The Bible Volume II.* Nashville: Thomas Nelson, 1983.

Pfeiffer, Charles F. and Everett F. Harrison, eds. *The Wycliffe Bible Commentary.* Nashville: The Southwestern Company, 1968.

Robinson, Haddon W. *Trusting the Shepherd: Insights from Psalm 23.* Grand Rapids: Discovery House Publishers, 2002.

Spargimino, Larry. *Digging Deeper.* Oklahoma City: Bible Belt Publishing, 2008.

The Holy Bible: King James Version. (electronic ed. of the 1769 edition of the 1611 Authorized Version). Bellingham WA: Logos Research Systems, Inc., 1995.

Towns, Elmer L. *Praying the 23rd Psalm.* Ventura, CA: Regal Books, 2001.

About the Author

James Collins currently serves as the Staff Evangelist for Southwest Radio Ministries. He served in various pastoral positions in Kansas, Oklahoma, Illinois, and California. Before being called to SWRC, James was a chaplain in the United States Army and served in Operation Enduring Freedom, Operation Iraqi Freedom, Operation New Dawn, and Operation Inherent Resolve.

A life-long learner, James has four graduate degrees including the Doctor of Ministry and the Doctor of Theology degrees. He loves reading, especially books on Bible prophecy.

James is married to the love of his life, Amanda Collins. They share their home with their three children, three dogs, and a lifetime collection of books.

James would love to hear from you. You can reach him by mail at PO Box 76834, Oklahoma City, OK 73147, or by email at info@swrc.com.

Also Available

Don't Throw The Believer Out With the Baptistry Water is a collection of *The Point Is ...,* the weekly newspaper column written by Pastor James Collins. Within these pages you will find the wit and wisdom of a country preacher. He is a natural-born storyteller with a talent for reducing everyday occurrences into messages that pack a spiritual punch. His stories have been called "modern-day parables."

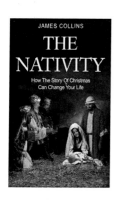

The Nativity was written to help you take a fresh look at the Christmas story—to help you see beyond the familiar and find the true Spirit of Christmas. Every year, millions of people around the globe celebrate Christmas. But what does it all mean? Drawing from both the Old and New Testaments, James Collins examines the most pivotal moment in human history—the birth of Jesus Christ. You will never look at the Christmas story the same way again.

Get your copies today at:
www.swrc.com